D0529333

Betty Crocker's

Cooking with American Wine

Prentice Hall Press

New York   London   Toronto   Sydney   Tokyo

Prentice Hall Press
Gulf + Western Building
One Gulf + Western Plaza
New York, NY 10023

Copyright © 1989 by General Mills, Inc.,
Minneapolis, Minnesota
All rights reserved, including the right of reproduction in whole
or in part in any form.

PRENTICE HALL PRESS and colophon are registered trade-
marks of Simon & Schuster, Inc.

BETTY CROCKER is a registered trademark of General Mills, Inc.

Library of Congress Cataloging-in-Publication Data
Crocker, Betty.
[Cooking with American wine]
Betty Crocker's cooking with American wine.—1st ed.
p.   cm.
Includes index.
ISBN 0-13-074295-3 : $12.95
1. Cookery (Wine)   2. Wine and wine making—United States.
I. Title.
TX726.C762   1989   88-22427
641.6′22—dc19   CIP

Manufactured in the United States of America

10   9   8   7   6   5   4   3   2   1

First Edition

Credits

GENERAL MILLS, INC.

Editor: Maureen Powers Fischer
Test Kitchen Home Economists: Mary Hallin Johnson, Mary Jane Friedhoff
Copy Editor: Susan Meyers
Editorial Assistant: Phyllis Weinbender
Food Stylists: Cindy Lund, Katie W. McElroy
Photographer: Nanci E. Doonan
Photography Assistant: Carolyn Luxmoore
Director, Betty Crocker Food and Publications Center: Marcia Copeland
Assistant Manager, Publications: Lois Tlusty

PRENTICE HALL PRESS

Vice-President and Associate Publisher: Anne Zeman
Senior Editor: Rebecca W. Atwater
Creative Director: J. C. Suarès
Designers: Patricia Fabricant, Suzanne Reisel
Prop Stylist: Janice Ervin
Illustrator: Nina Duran

Contents

INTRODUCTION

Cheers!

Why bring you a book on cooking with *American* wine? For three reasons. First, we always advocate cooking with local ingredients; they are easy to find, usually reasonably priced and in optimal condition—wonderful for quick inspiration!

Second, there is every reason to be proud of American wines. Our wine industry struggled in the years that followed the repeal of prohibition laws; it was a time of nurturing vineyards and exhaustive study of European techniques. Those were years of backbreaking work, and they produced extraordinary results. Today American wines, in all their diversity, are among the world's finest.

Finally, we wanted to make it easy to cook with American wine, and that means cooking with confidence. The experience and expertise of Betty Crocker kitchens bring you recipes that were created with you in mind.

Cooking with wine doesn't have to be intimidating, and with this book in hand, we're sure you will agree. Here's to your tour of American wine country!

THE BETTY CROCKER EDITORS

Cooking with Wine

American wine-making, an industry more than two hundred years old, has come into its own. Once considered upstarts of dubious quality, today American wines are judged side by side with the best that wine makers around the world can offer. Why cook with American wine? Wine enhances the taste of food, as anyone who has enjoyed a glass of crisp Chardonnay can attest. In cooking, wine adds a wonderful dimension to the flavor of a dish.

When wine is heated, the alcohol in it evaporates. This means when wine is added to a stew, the alcohol virtually disappears while the stew cooks, leaving behind the subtle flavor of the wine. Wine can be used to flavor already-cooked foods (as some desserts) or, in the case of marinades, to flavor foods even before they are cooked. You don't need to use an expensive wine in cooking, but it should be one you could enjoy sipping on its own.

The recipes in this book call for table wines. There are commercially produced cooking wines, but salts and other flavoring agents have been added to them. This makes them unsuitable for drinking. Furthermore, there is only a handful of cooking wines to choose from, compared with the vast selection of wines made for the glass. The fun of cooking with wine is letting your imagination soar. Use these recipes as guidelines for both the type of wine and how much of it to use, and then experiment. If you add wine to a dish, substitute it for part of the liquid ingredients. For example, try replacing one-half cup of broth with wine in one of your favorite recipes. Taste food cooked with wine before reaching for the salt shaker (you might need less salt than you think), and bear in mind that very spicy or sour dishes are among the few that wine doesn't improve.

In addition to table wines, fortified wines and wine coolers are used in some of our recipes. Fortified wines (sherry, Madeira and port) are given an extra boost of alcohol before bottling. They are sipped at room temperature, generally before or after (not with) dinner. Wine coolers are relative newcomers. Mixtures of fruit juice, wine and flavorings, they are lower in alcohol than wine and are best drunk icy cold.

Wine Label Know-how
A wine label is obviously your best source of information about a bottle's contents and how the wine will taste. American labeling follows closely the conventions of the European wine industry; however, American wines are not identified by vineyard (as European wines so frequently are), but by the type of wine (or grape) and the name of the producer.

Wine is generic or varietal. Generic American wines, made in the style of their European counterparts, do not have to be made from a particular grape. A winemaker may blend several grapes to make a generic wine to his taste. Burgundy, Moselle and Chablis are examples of generic wines. Varietal wines are named for the grape from which they are principally made. Federal law stipulates that a wine may take a varietal name if 75 percent or more of the grapes used were that variety of grape. Cabernet Sauvignon, Grey Riesling, Chardonnay and Sémillon are names of grape varieties and also of the wines made from them.

Deciphering a Label
Generally speaking, an informative and specific wine label is an indication that care has been taken to produce a good wine.

American wine is now sold in metric quantities. The volume is printed on the wine label or on the bottle itself.

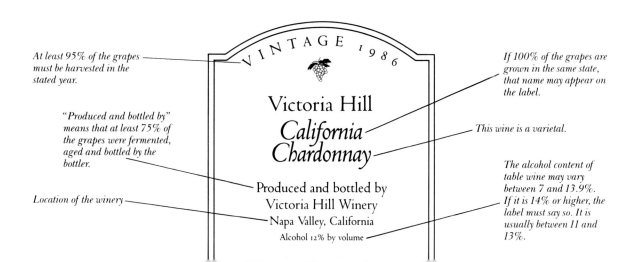

At least 95% of the grapes must be harvested in the stated year.

"Produced and bottled by" means that at least 75% of the grapes were fermented, aged and bottled by the bottler.

Location of the winery

VINTAGE 1986

Victoria Hill
California
Chardonnay

Produced and bottled by
Victoria Hill Winery
Napa Valley, California
Alcohol 12% by volume

If 100% of the grapes are grown in the same state, that name may appear on the label.

This wine is a varietal.

The alcohol content of table wine may vary between 7 and 13.9%. If it is 14% or higher, the label must say so. It is usually between 11 and 13%.

Metric Volume	Approximate Measure
375 milliliters	1½ cups
750 milliliters	3 cups
1 liter	4 cups
1½ liters	6 cups

Choosing a Wine

What wine should you drink with your meal? Purists insist on drinking the same wine that goes into the cooking pot. Others claim that the flavor of the wine in the food has been altered by the cooking process and may no longer be "compatible with itself." Taste your food and rely on your own opinions. On special occasions, you may want to drink the same kind of wine you used in cooking, but a wine of better quality. What will serve you well in times of doubt is the old rule of thumb: White wine is traditional with seafood, veal and poultry; red with darker meats; and rosé is pleasant when a wide assortment of different foods is served at one time, as for a buffet or picnic. Or, think of it this way: Strong wine complements strong food.

Serving Wine

If served too cold, wine has little flavor. Rosé and white wine taste best if served at around 40 to 55 degrees, red around 60 to 65 degrees. Cold champagne is sparkling and delicious, but if chilled below 35 degrees its effervescent nature is diminished. As for wine glasses, an 8-ounce glass is all-purpose. Never over-fill wine glasses; leave some space in the glass so that the aroma of the wine can be enjoyed.

Storing Wine

Wine should be stored in a cool, dark place. It keeps best in an unopened bottle. As soon as wine is exposed to oxygen, its flavor begins to change. This may be desirable, as when a bottle of red wine is opened and allowed to "breathe" briefly before it is poured. In some cases, particularly in the case of young, astringent red wines, breathing can soften a harsh wine considerably.

The quality of leftover wine in its partly empty bottle decreases as time goes by. Consider decanting leftover wine into a small, scrupulously clean container with a tight-fitting cover. Otherwise you can leave the wine in its bottle and keep track of the days. A bottle three-quarters full will probably be as delicious three to five days after opening, and a half-full bottle two to three days; a less-than-half-full bottle is best used within a day or two.

American Wine

Approximately 90 percent of American wine is produced in California. But, if you venture beyond the success of California wines and give locally produced wines a try, you will not be disappointed. Frequently, wines made in local, little-known wineries are good bargains, and sometimes they are unexpected masterpieces. There are commercial vineyards in more than thirty-six states, from Washington to New Mexico to Florida, and just about everywhere in between. Happily, with just a little effort, you will find wines that please you in every price range. As you discover marvelous new wines, we hope that this book will help you explore the pleasure of bringing them into your kitchen.

Cooking with American Wine

American Wine

White Wine

VARIETAL: Angelica,* Chardonnay (Pinot Chardonnay), Chenin Blanc (White Pinot), Dry (white) Vermouth, Emerald Riesling, French Colombard, Gewürztraminer, Green Hungarian, Grey Riesling, Muscadet, Pinot Blanc, Riesling (White Riesling, Johannisberg Riesling), Sauvignon Blanc (Fumé Blanc), Sémillon, Sylvaner Riesling, Traminer.

GENERIC: Chablis, Haut (sweet) Sauterne,* Lake Country White, Moselle, Mountain White, Muscatel,* Rhine Wine, Sauterne (dry), Tokay,* White Burgundy, White Kosher Wine, White Muscat.

Red Wine

VARIETAL: Baco Noir, Barbera, Cabernet Sauvignon, Catawba Red, Charbono, Gamay, Gamay Beaujolais, Grenache, Grignolino, Merlot, Petite Sirah, Pinot Noir, Pinot St. George, Ruby Cabernet, Sweet (red) Vermouth,* Syrah, Zinfandel.

GENERIC: Barberone, Burgundy, Chianti, Claret, Concord, Lake Country Red, Vino Rosso.

Rosé or Blush Wine

VARIETAL: Blush Chablis, Cabernet Blanc (White Cabernet Sauvignon), Gamay Rosé, Grenache Rosé, Grignolino Rosé, Petite Sirah Blanc, Pinot Noir Blanc, White Zinfandel.

GENERIC: Pink Chablis, Rosé, Vin Rosé.

Sparkling Wine

CHAMPAGNE: Natural (very dry), Brut (dry), Extra Dry (somewhat dry), Dry,* Sec* (sweeter than dry), Demi-sec* (sweeter than sec).

ROSÉ OR BLUSH: Crackling Rosé,* Pink Champagne.*

RED WINE: Cold Duck,* Sparkling Burgundy.*

Fortified and Dessert Wines

Madeira,* Marsala,* Port* (Ruby, Tawny, Tinta, White), Sherry (Cocktail, Cream,* Dry).

* SWEET

CHAPTER 1

Poultry Pleasers

Country-style Chicken Casserole

3- to 3½-pound broiler-fryer chicken
⅛ teaspoon pepper
2 tablespoons margarine or butter
4 thin strips salt pork or 4 slices bacon
8 medium carrots, cut into fourths
8 medium turnips, cut into fourths, or 8 small whole white onions
2 tablespoons margarine or butter, melted
1 can (10¾ ounces) condensed chicken broth
¼ teaspoon salt
⅛ teaspoon pepper
½ cup Pinot Blanc or dry white wine
1 tablespoon plus 1½ teaspoons cornstarch
3 tablespoons cold water

Rub skin of chicken with ⅛ teaspoon pepper. Fold wings across back with tips touching; tie drumsticks to tail.

Melt 2 tablespoons margarine in 4-quart Dutch oven. Add chicken and cook over medium heat about 30 minutes. Place 2 strips salt pork over breasts and 1 strip lengthwise over each drumstick.

Heat oven to 325°. Place carrots and turnips in Dutch oven around chicken. Drizzle with melted margarine. Pour broth over chicken and vegetables; sprinkle with salt and ⅛ teaspoon pepper. Cover and bake until thickest pieces of chicken are done, about 1¾ hours.

Remove chicken and vegetables to warm platter. Remove salt pork strips and string from chicken; keep chicken warm.

Stir wine into chicken broth. Heat to boiling, stirring constantly. Boil and stir 3 minutes. Mix cornstarch and water; stir into wine mixture. Heat to boiling over medium heat, stirring constantly. Boil and stir 3 minutes; skim off fat. Serve sauce with chicken.

6 servings.

Grilled Chicken

2¹/₂-pound broiler-fryer chicken, cut up
³/₄ cup Gamay Beaujolais or dry red wine
¹/₄ cup lemon juice
1 tablespoon instant minced onion
¹/₂ teaspoon aromatic bitters
¹/₄ teaspoon salt

Place chicken pieces in shallow glass dish or plastic bag. Mix remaining ingredients; pour over chicken pieces. Cover and refrigerate at least 1 hour.

Remove chicken; reserve wine mixture. Cover and grill chicken, bone sides down, 5 to 6 inches from medium coals 15 to 20 minutes; turn chicken. Cover and grill, turning and brushing 2 or 3 times with wine mixture, until thickest pieces are done, 20 to 40 minutes longer.

6 servings.

BROILED CHICKEN: Prepare as directed above except set oven control to broil. Place chicken, skin sides down, on rack in broiler pan. Broil with tops 5 to 7 inches from heat, brushing with wine mixture every 10 to 15 minutes and turning chicken as it browns, until thickest pieces are done, 40 to 50 minutes.

Chicken with Tarragon

1 cup chicken broth or bouillon
1 tablespoon snipped fresh tarragon leaves or 1 teaspoon dried
  tarragon leaves
¹/₂ teaspoon salt
¹/₈ teaspoon pepper
3- to 3¹/₂-pound broiler-fryer chicken, cut up
3 medium carrots, sliced
1 bay leaf
4 ounces mushrooms, sliced
2 stalks celery, sliced
1 medium onion, sliced
¹/₂ cup Chenin Blanc or dry white wine
¹/₂ cup half-and-half
3 tablespoons all-purpose flour
1 egg yolk
Hot cooked noodles

*B*itters are concentrated essences flavored principally with herbs. Their origins are medicinal, but today we tend to use them for their complex, mysterious flavors. Bitters may be made with such unlikely sounding ingredients as gentian, wormwood and tree bark. Just a dash or two in a sauce (or cocktail) will suffice.

Heat chicken broth, tarragon, salt, pepper, chicken, carrots and bay leaf to boiling in 12-inch skillet or 4-quart Dutch oven; reduce heat. Cover and simmer 30 minutes. Add mushrooms, celery and onion. Heat to boiling; reduce heat. Cover and simmer until thickest pieces of chicken are done, about 15 minutes.

Remove chicken and vegetables to warm platter; keep warm. Drain liquid from skillet; strain and reserve 1 cup. Pour reserved liquid and the wine into skillet. Mix half-and-half, flour and egg yolk until smooth; stir into wine mixture. Cook, stirring constantly, until thickened. Serve with chicken, vegetables and noodles.

6 servings.

Orange-Ginger Chicken

3- to 3¹/₂-pound broiler-fryer chicken, cut up
2 tablespoons vegetable oil
2 teaspoons finely shredded orange peel
1 cup orange juice
1 cup Pinot Blanc or dry white wine
¹/₃ cup honey
2 tablespoons cornstarch
2 teaspoons grated gingerroot or ¹/₂ teaspoon ground ginger
¹/₄ teaspoon salt
Hot cooked bulgur or barley

Cook chicken in hot oil in 12-inch skillet or 4-quart Dutch oven over medium heat until brown, about 15 minutes; drain.

Mix remaining ingredients except bulgur. Pour over chicken in skillet. Heat to boiling; reduce heat. Cover and simmer until thickest pieces of chicken are done, about 40 minutes. Serve with bulgur. Garnish with orange slices if desired.

6 servings.

*F*irst imported to western Europe from Malabar and Bengal, ginger is widely grown. The root of this tropical plant is used both fresh and as a dry ground powder. When fresh ginger is called for, peel off the thin skin before proceeding to chop, mince or grate the root. Preserved ginger, usually candied in syrup, and crystallized ginger (no syrup) are delicious, pungent additions to many dishes.

Chicken in Red Wine

6 slices bacon
3- to 3½-pound broiler-fryer chicken, cut up
4 medium potatoes, cut into fourths
12 small onions
8 ounces mushrooms, sliced
1 clove garlic, crushed
Bouquet Garni*
½ teaspoon salt
1 cup Pinot Noir or dry red wine
1 cup hot water
2 tablespoons all-purpose flour
3 tablespoons cold water
Snipped parsley

Cook bacon in 4-quart Dutch oven until crisp. Remove bacon; drain, crumble and reserve. Cook half of the chicken in hot fat over medium heat until brown, about 20 minutes. Repeat with remaining chicken. Drain fat.

Place chicken, potatoes, onions, mushrooms, garlic, bouquet garni, salt and reserved bacon in Dutch oven. Pour wine and hot water over chicken and vegetables. Heat to boiling; reduce heat. Cover and simmer until chicken is done, 35 to 40 minutes.

Remove bouquet garni. Remove chicken and vegetables to warm platter; keep warm. Shake flour and cold water in tightly covered container; gradually stir into cooking liquid. Heat to boiling, stirring constantly. Boil and stir 1 minute. Pour sauce over chicken. Sprinkle with parsley.

6 servings.

*Place 2 large sprigs parsley, 1 bay leaf and ½ teaspoon dried thyme leaves in cheesecloth bag; tie securely.

*T*his is the *Coq au Vin* so loved by the French. *Bouquet garni* is something else we've borrowed from the French. It's a small bundle of aromatics all tied up together (sometimes wrapped in cheesecloth) so that it can be easily retrieved and discarded before serving. A bouquet garni flavors a dish while it cooks and always includes bay leaf, parsley and thyme or rosemary.

Chicken in Red Wine

Hearty Chicken Soup

3- to 3 1/2-pound broiler-fryer chicken, cut up
2 tablespoons vegetable oil
2 large onions, thinly sliced and separated into rings
2 cloves garlic, finely chopped
1 cup Gewürztraminer or dry white wine
1 cup water
1 tablespoon sugar
*1 tablespoon snipped fresh thyme leaves or 1 teaspoon dried thyme
    leaves*
1/4 teaspoon salt
1/4 teaspoon pepper
1 can (16 ounces) whole tomatoes, undrained
1 can (10 3/4 ounces) condensed chicken broth
1 medium green bell pepper, cut into 1/4-inch strips
6 slices French bread, toasted
Snipped parsley

Remove skin and any excess fat from chicken pieces. Heat oil in 4-quart Dutch oven. Cook chicken in hot oil until brown on all sides; remove chicken.

Cook and stir onions and garlic in Dutch oven until onions are tender. Return chicken to Dutch oven; add remaining ingredients except bell pepper, French bread and parsley. Break up tomatoes. Heat to boiling; reduce heat. Cover and simmer until thickest pieces of chicken are done, about 1 hour.

Skim fat from chicken mixture. Add bell pepper. Heat to boiling; reduce heat. Cover and simmer just until bell pepper is tender, about 10 minutes. Place a slice of French bread in each of 6 serving bowls. Spoon chicken and broth over bread. Sprinkle with parsley.

6 servings.

*U*se your favorite chicken pieces in any of the recipes calling for cut-up broiler-fryer chicken—just substitute the same weight of chicken pieces. Drumsticks, thighs and breasts may cost more per pound but they have more meat. And you get just what you like, light or dark, in the bargain!

Barbecued Chicken

8 chicken drumsticks or 2 pounds chicken pieces
1 medium onion, thinly sliced and separated into rings
½ cup Gamay Beaujolais or dry red wine
½ cup chili sauce
2 tablespoons packed brown sugar
¼ teaspoon red pepper sauce
1 clove garlic, finely chopped

Heat oven to 375°. Remove skin from chicken drumsticks. Arrange onion in ungreased rectangular baking dish, 11 × 7 × 1½ inches. Place chicken on onion. Mix remaining ingredients; pour over chicken. Bake uncovered until chicken is done, 50 to 60 minutes, spooning sauce over chicken after 30 minutes.

4 servings.

Spicy Chicken Wings

8 chicken wings (about 1¾ pounds)
½ cup Sémillon or dry white wine
½ teaspoon dry mustard
½ teaspoon ground red pepper
½ teaspoon paprika
½ teaspoon ground cumin
⅛ teaspoon salt
⅛ teaspoon pepper
Several drops red pepper sauce

Put chicken wings in saucepan and cover with water. Heat to boiling; reduce heat. Cover and simmer 10 minutes; drain. Arrange wings in ungreased square pan, 8 × 8 × 2 inches.

Heat oven to 375°. Mix remaining ingredients. Brush wings generously with mixture. Bake uncovered until wings are golden brown, about 25 minutes.

4 servings.

Spicy Chicken Wings can be served as the ultimate informal appetizer; trim wing tips and cut each wing in half before cooking. Serve with plenty of napkins.

Chicken with Figs in Port Sauce

2 large whole chicken breasts (about 2 pounds)
2 tablespoons margarine or butter
1 cup Tawny Port or sweet red wine
½ cup whipping cream
¼ cup sliced green onions (with tops)
1 tablespoon finely shredded orange peel
6 sun-dried figs, cut into fourths
6 slices bacon, crisply cooked and crumbled
Hot cooked rice

Remove skin and bones from chicken breasts; cut each whole chicken breast into halves. Flatten each half breast to ½-inch thickness between plastic wrap or waxed paper, being careful not to tear chicken.

Heat margarine in 10-inch skillet over medium heat until melted. Cook chicken in margarine, turning once, until light brown, 15 to 20 minutes. Add port. Heat to boiling; reduce heat. Cover and simmer until chicken is done, 15 to 20 minutes. Remove chicken to warm platter; keep warm.

Add whipping cream to skillet. Heat to boiling; cook uncovered until very thick, about 8 minutes. Stir in remaining ingredients except rice. Cook, stirring occasionally, until figs are hot, about 3 minutes. Place chicken pieces on rice; spoon sauce over chicken and rice. Garnish with orange sections and sprigs of fresh herb if desired.

4 servings.

CHICKEN WITH APRICOT SAUCE: Substitute ½ cup snipped dried apricots for the figs. Garnish with apricot halves and sprigs of fresh herb if desired.

Simply luxurious, this dish combines Tawny Port, heavy cream and figs in a richly flavored sauce. Marvelous "company food," you'll want to serve this with a spoon so guests can savor every drop. For a decidedly different variation, substitute dried apricots for the figs.

Chicken with Figs in Port Sauce

Cooking with American Wine

Four-Cheese Chicken Rolls

2 large whole chicken breasts (about 2 pounds)
1/2 cup shredded mozzarella cheese (2 ounces)
1/2 cup shredded provolone cheese (2 ounces)
1/3 cup ricotta or dry cottage cheese
2 tablespoons snipped parsley
1/2 cup Johannisberg Riesling or dry white wine
1 container (8 ounces) soft cream cheese with chives and onions
1/2 cup Johannisberg Riesling or dry white wine
1 tablespoon snipped parsley

Remove skin and bones from chicken breasts; cut each whole chicken breast into halves. Flatten each half breast to 1/4-inch thickness between plastic wrap or waxed paper, being careful not to tear chicken.

Heat oven to 400°. Mix mozzarella, provolone and ricotta cheeses and 2 tablespoons snipped parsley. Place about 1/4 cup cheese mixture on one end of each chicken breast half. Roll up; secure with wooden picks. Place rolls in ungreased square baking dish, 8 × 8 × 2 inches. Pour 1/2 cup wine over chicken. Bake uncovered, brushing chicken with wine occasionally, until chicken is done, about 40 minutes.

Heat remaining ingredients over low heat, stirring frequently, until cream cheese is melted and mixture is hot. Pour 1/2 cup cheese mixture over chicken; serve with remaining cheese mixture. Serve over spinach noodles if desired.

4 servings.

This is a genuine palate-pleaser. Four different cheeses are used to stuff and blanket chicken breasts. The marriage of their distinctive flavors is rich and satisfying.

Pork-stuffed Chicken Rolls

3 large whole chicken breasts (about 3 pounds)
1/2 pound ground pork
1 small onion, finely chopped
1 clove garlic, finely chopped
1/2 cup soft bread crumbs (about 1/2 slice bread)
1/4 teaspoon salt
1/4 teaspoon ground savory
1/4 teaspoon pepper
1 egg, beaten
2 tablespoons margarine or butter, melted
1/2 cup Grey Riesling or dry white wine
1/2 cup cold water
2 teaspoons cornstarch
1/2 teaspoon instant chicken bouillon

These chicken rolls are filled with a moist, savory-scented stuffing. Savory, an herb seldom called for, has an assertive flavor that marries superbly with the strong flavor of pork.

Cooking with American Wine

Remove skin and bones from chicken breasts; cut each whole chicken breast into halves. Flatten each half breast to ¼-inch thickness between plastic wrap or waxed paper, being careful not to tear chicken.

Heat oven to 400°. Cook and stir ground pork, onion and garlic in 10-inch skillet over medium heat until pork is brown; drain. Stir in bread crumbs, salt, savory, pepper and egg. Place about ⅓ cup pork mixture on one end of each chicken breast half. Roll up; secure with wooden picks. Place rolls in buttered rectangular baking dish, 11 × 7 × 1½ inches. Brush rolls with melted margarine; pour any remaining margarine over rolls. Add wine. Bake uncovered until chicken is done, 35 to 40 minutes.

Remove chicken to warm platter; remove wooden picks. Keep warm. Pour liquid from baking dish into 1-quart saucepan. Mix water and cornstarch; stir into liquid. Stir in bouillon (dry). Heat to boiling over medium heat, stirring constantly. Boil and stir 1 minute. Pour over chicken. Top with snipped parsley if desired.

6 servings.

Sherried Chicken Breasts

2 medium whole chicken breasts (about 1½ pounds)
¼ cup soy sauce
¼ cup Medium-dry Sherry or dry white wine
1 tablespoon sugar
1 tablespoon vegetable oil
1 teaspoon grated gingerroot or ¼ teaspoon ground ginger
1 clove garlic, crushed

Remove skin and bones from chicken breasts; cut each chicken breast into halves. Place chicken in a shallow glass dish or plastic bag. Mix remaining ingredients; pour over chicken. Cover and refrigerate at least 1 hour.

Remove chicken; reserve sherry mixture. Cover and grill chicken 5 to 6 inches from medium coals 10 to 20 minutes; turn chicken. Cover and grill, turning and brushing 2 or 3 times with sherry mixture, until done, 10 to 20 minutes.

4 servings.

Broiled Sherried Chicken Breasts: Prepare as directed above except set oven control to broil. Place chicken on rack in broiler pan. Broil with tops about 4 inches from heat 5 minutes; turn. Brush with sherry mixture; broil until chicken is done, 5 to 6 minutes longer.

Couscous-stuffed Chicken Breasts

2 large whole chicken breasts (about 2 pounds)
¾ cup Apple-Cranberry Wine Cooler or Red Wine Cooler
⅔ cup couscous
⅓ cup raisins
¼ cup chopped green onions (with tops)
¼ teaspoon salt
⅛ teaspoon ground cinnamon
1 package (3 ounces) cream cheese, cut into cubes
¾ cup Apple-Cranberry Wine Cooler or Red Wine Cooler
1 tablespoon cold water
1 teaspoon cornstarch

Remove bones from chicken breasts; cut each whole chicken breast into halves. Heat ¾ cup wine cooler to boiling in 2-quart saucepan. Stir in couscous, raisins, green onions, salt and cinnamon. Remove from heat and let stand until all wine is absorbed, 2 to 3 minutes. Stir in cream cheese. Cook and stir over low heat until cream cheese is melted.

Heat oven to 350°. Loosen skin from cut side of each chicken breast half, using a sharp knife to form a pocket. Spoon about ½ cup couscous mixture into each pocket; secure with wooden picks. Place chicken in ungreased rectangular baking dish, 12 × 7½ × 2 inches. Pour ¾ cup wine cooler over chicken. Bake uncovered until chicken is done, 35 to 40 minutes. Remove chicken to warm platter and remove wooden picks; keep chicken warm.

Pour ⅓ cup of the cooking liquid into 1-quart saucepan. Mix water and cornstarch; stir into liquid. Heat to boiling over medium heat, stirring constantly. Boil and stir 1 minute. Serve with chicken.

4 servings.

*C*ouscous, a Moroccan and Middle Eastern staple, is made from semolina wheat and has a ricelike texture. Traditionally steamed in a basket set over the main dish, the couscous grains are cooked by the steam that rises from the bubbling stew below. Couscous is an ideal base for poultry stuffing; the semolina readily absorbs the cooking juices.

Couscous-stuffed Chicken Breasts

Stuffed Breast of Chicken

3- to 3½-pound broiler-fryer chicken, cut up
2 slices white bread, torn into pieces
6 sprigs parsley
½ teaspoon salt
¼ teaspoon pepper
¼ teaspoon ground savory
1 egg, beaten
2 tablespoons margarine or butter, melted
1 cup Grey Riesling or dry white wine
½ cup cold water
1 tablespoon cornstarch
1 teaspoon instant chicken bouillon

Remove skin and any excess fat from chicken thighs, drumsticks, wings and back, using sharp knife; reserve thigh skin. Cut meat from thighs, drumsticks, wings and back. Place meat in workbowl of food processor fitted with steel blade. Cover and process until ground. Add bread, parsley, salt, pepper, savory and egg. Process until well blended.

Heat oven to 400°. Remove bones from chicken breasts. Cut each chicken breast into halves. Loosen skin from cut side of each chicken breast half, using a sharp knife to form a pocket. Fill pocket with stuffing; fold skin down to cover stuffing. Use reserved skin to cover stuffing if necessary.

Place chicken in buttered rectangular baking dish, 11 × 7 × 1½ inches. Brush with melted margarine. Pour wine over chicken. Bake uncovered until chicken is done, about 35 minutes. Remove chicken to warm platter; keep warm.

Pour liquid from baking dish into 1-quart saucepan. Mix water and cornstarch; stir into liquid. Stir in bouillon (dry). Heat to boiling over medium heat, stirring constantly. Boil and stir 1 minute. Pour sauce over chicken.

4 servings.

Lemony Chicken

6 small chicken breast halves (about 2 pounds)
¼ cup margarine or butter
½ cup Gewürztraminer or dry white wine
1 tablespoon lemon juice
¼ teaspoon salt
½ teaspoon snipped fresh dill weed or ⅛ teaspoon dried dill weed
½ lemon, thinly sliced
2 tablespoons sliced green onions (with tops)

Remove skin and bones from chicken breast halves. Cook chicken in margarine in 10-inch skillet, turning once, until chicken is light brown, about 5 minutes on each side.

Mix wine, lemon juice, salt and dill weed; pour over chicken. Place lemon slices on chicken. Heat to boiling; reduce heat. Cover and simmer until chicken is done, 10 to 15 minutes. Remove chicken to warm platter; keep warm.

Heat wine mixture to boiling; cook until reduced by half, about 3 minutes. Pour over chicken; sprinkle with green onions.

6 servings.

Hot and Creamy Chicken Croissants

4 croissants, split lengthwise into halves
1 cup sliced mushrooms
3 tablespoons margarine or butter
1 tablespoon all-purpose flour
¼ teaspoon garlic salt
½ cup milk
¼ cup Grey Riesling or dry white wine
1 cup cut-up cooked chicken
½ cup shredded process Swiss cheese (2 ounces)
1 jar (6 ounces) marinated artichoke hearts, drained and cut into
  halves

Heat oven to 300°. Heat croissant halves on ungreased cookie sheet about 10 minutes. Cook and stir mushrooms in 2 tablespoons margarine in 1½-quart saucepan over medium heat until tender, 2 to 3 minutes. Remove mushrooms, using slotted spoon; reserve.

Heat remaining 1 tablespoon margarine in same saucepan until melted; stir in flour and garlic salt. Cook, stirring constantly, until bubbly; remove from heat. Stir in milk and wine. Heat to boiling, stirring constantly. Boil and stir 1 minute. Stir in reserved mushrooms, chicken, cheese and artichoke hearts; heat through. Spoon mixture over bottom halves of croissants; top with remaining croissant halves.

4 servings.

If you purchase chicken breasts already skinned and boned, you can prepare this dish in a flash.

Chicken and Fettuccine with Dijon Sauce

Dijon, an influential (and once powerful) city in the old French province of Burgundy, is famous for the mustards produced there. You may be sure that any dish described as "Dijon" is flavored with prepared mustard.

If you don't have cooked chicken or turkey on hand, substitute canned chicken in any recipe calling for cooked chicken in small pieces. One 5-ounce can of chunk chicken yields about ⅔ cup chicken pieces.

6 ounces uncooked spinach fettuccine
½ cup chopped onion
2 cloves garlic, crushed
2 tablespoons margarine or butter
1 cup milk
½ cup Chardonnay or dry white wine
2 tablespoons snipped parsley
2 tablespoons Dijon-style mustard
1 package (3 ounces) cream cheese with chives, cut into cubes
1½ cups cut-up cooked chicken or turkey

Cook fettuccine as directed on package; drain. Cook and stir onion and garlic in margarine over medium heat in 3-quart saucepan until onion is tender. Add remaining ingredients except chicken; stir until cream cheese is melted. Add chicken and hot fettuccine to cheese mixture; toss until evenly coated. Heat just until hot. Garnish with chives and freshly ground pepper if desired.

4 servings.

Chicken and Fettuccine with Dijon Sauce

Cornish Hens with Corn Bread Stuffing

4 Rock Cornish hens (about 1 pound each)
½ cup Chenin Blanc or dry white wine
¼ cup orange juice
½ cup chopped celery
¼ cup finely chopped onion
2 tablespoons snipped parsley
¼ teaspoon ground sage
¼ teaspoon salt
⅛ teaspoon pepper
¼ cup margarine or butter
4 cups crumbled corn bread
2 tablespoons Chenin Blanc or dry white wine

Place Cornish hens in a large plastic bag. Pour in ½ cup wine and the orange juice. Fasten bag securely. Refrigerate at least 2 hours but no longer than 24 hours, turning bag twice. Remove hens; reserve wine mixture.

Heat oven to 375°. Cook and stir celery, onion, parsley, sage, salt and pepper in margarine in 2-quart saucepan until celery is tender; remove from heat. Stir in remaining ingredients. Spoon about 1 cup corn bread stuffing into each hen. Secure opening with skewer. Tie legs together with string. Place hens, breast sides up, on rack in shallow roasting pan. Roast uncovered, brushing with wine mixture occasionally, until thickest pieces are done, about 1 hour.

4 servings.

*W*e most often associate sage-scented stuffing with turkey. Here, the little birds get their turn for an amusing change of pace. You may substitute a 3½-pound broiler-fryer chicken for the Cornish hens. In that case, roast uncovered at 375° for about 1¾ hours.

Cornish Hens with Corn Bread Stuffing

Spicy Cornish Hens

¼ teaspoon ground cloves
¼ teaspoon ground nutmeg
¼ teaspoon pepper
¼ teaspoon ground thyme
4 Rock Cornish hens (about 1 pound each)
4 slices bacon, cut into halves
1¼ cups Zinfandel or dry red wine
½ cup boiling water
2 tablespoons finely chopped onion
2 tablespoons snipped parsley
½ teaspoon instant chicken bouillon
3 to 4 cups hot cooked brown or white rice
⅓ cup currant jelly

Heat oven to 350°. Mix cloves, nutmeg, pepper and thyme; rub on outsides and in cavities of Cornish hens. Place hens, breast sides up, on rack in shallow roasting pan. Crisscross bacon slices over hens. Mix remaining ingredients except rice and currant jelly; pour into roasting pan.

Bake uncovered 1 hour. Increase oven temperature to 400°. Bake until thickest pieces of hens are done, about 10 minutes longer.

Remove hens to warm platter; keep warm. Remove bacon and cut into small pieces; stir into rice. Strain hot juices from roasting pan into 1½-quart saucepan; stir in currant jelly. Heat mixture over medium heat, stirring constantly, until jelly has melted; skim off fat. Arrange rice around hens on platter; spoon sauce over hens.

4 servings.

Turkey in Patty Shells

½ package (16-ounce size) frozen mixed vegetables
2 tablespoons margarine or butter
¼ cup all-purpose flour
½ teaspoon salt
¼ teaspoon pepper
1¼ cups milk
2 cups cut-up cooked turkey or chicken
½ cup Pinot Blanc or dry white wine
4 baked patty shells

Cook frozen vegetables in 2-quart saucepan as directed on package; drain. Stir in margarine over low heat until melted. Stir in flour, salt and pepper; remove from heat. Gradually stir in milk. Heat to boiling over medium heat, stirring constantly. Boil and stir 1 minute. Stir in turkey and wine; heat through. Spoon mixture into patty shells.

4 servings.

Walnut-stuffed Turkey

3 medium onions, finely chopped
¾ cup margarine or butter
3 cups unseasoned croutons
2 cups chopped walnuts
¾ cup raisins
1 cup Chardonnay or dry white wine
¼ to ½ cup water, as desired
1½ teaspoons ground sage
1¼ teaspoons salt
2 large stalks celery, chopped
10- to 12-pound turkey
2 tablespoons margarine or butter, melted
1 cup Chardonnay or dry white wine
1 teaspoon instant chicken bouillon
1 cup boiling water

Cook and stir onions in ¾ cup margarine in 4-quart Dutch oven until tender; remove from heat. Stir in croutons, walnuts, raisins, 1 cup wine, ¼ to ½ cup water (depending on desired moistness of stuffing), the sage, salt and celery. Stuff turkey just before baking.

Heat oven to 325°. Place turkey, breast side up, on rack in shallow roasting pan. Brush with 2 tablespoons margarine. Pour 1 cup wine over turkey. Dissolve bouillon (dry) in 1 cup boiling water; pour over turkey. Insert meat thermometer so tip is in thickest part of inside thigh muscle or breast meat and does not touch bone.

Bake uncovered until thermometer registers 185° or until drumstick can be moved easily, 4 to 4½ hours. Place aluminum foil loosely over turkey when it begins to turn golden. When the turkey is done, remove from oven and let stand 20 minutes for easier carving.

10 servings.

*C*hardonnay, a distinguished varietal white wine, brings a subtle fruitiness to this walnut-rich stuffing. Chardonnay is generally acclaimed for soft, full flavor. The ripeness of the grapes determines just how sweet the wine can be. But what is true for most wines is true for Chardonnay; though the type of grape dictates the type of wine, the flavor is in the hands of the winemaker.

*S*esame oil can have either a pale or dark gold color. The pale oil has a subtle flavor. The dark oil is made from seeds that have been roasted and tastes very strongly of sesame and is used primarily as a flavoring.

*M*ost commercial chutneys are made principally with mangoes, but every enthusiast of Indian cookery has a favorite recipe. Chutneys are made with tamarinds, apples, peaches, pickled limes and lemons, green tomatoes and pears. Then, cooks choose among garlic, shallots, cardamom, red pepper, cloves, ginger, coriander, as well as mustard, celery and cumin seeds to season their chutney.

Oriental Broth with Turkey

Oriental Broth with Turkey

1 pound ground turkey
1 egg
½ cup dry bread crumbs
1½ teaspoons finely chopped gingerroot
¼ teaspoon salt
¼ teaspoon pepper
1 tablespoon sesame or vegetable oil
2 large stalks bok choy (with leaves)
2 carrots, thinly sliced
1 cup Sémillon or dry white wine
2 cans (14½ ounces each) chicken broth

Mix ground turkey, egg, bread crumbs, gingerroot, salt and pepper. Shape mixture into 1-inch balls. Cook in oil in 4-quart Dutch oven over medium heat, turning frequently, until brown, about 10 minutes.

Separate bok choy leaves from stalks. Cut leaves into thin strips; reserve. Cut stalks into ¼-inch slices. Add bok choy stalks, carrots, wine and chicken broth to meatballs in Dutch oven. Heat to boiling; reduce heat. Cover and simmer until vegetables are crisp-tender, about 20 minutes. Stir in reserved bok choy leaves and cook just until wilted.

6 servings.

Duckling with Chutney Sauce

4- to 4½-pound duckling
½ cup Chenin Blanc or dry white wine
1 tablespoon margarine or butter, melted
¼ teaspoon ground ginger
½ cup unsweetened applesauce
½ cup chutney
¼ cup raisins

Heat oven to 350°. Fasten skin of duckling to back, using skewers. Prick skin several times with fork. Place duckling, breast side up, on rack in shallow roasting pan. Mix wine, margarine and ginger. Brush duckling with wine mixture. Roast, brushing with wine mixture and removing excess fat from pan occasionally, until done, about 2 hours. Let stand 10 minutes for easier carving.

Heat remaining wine mixture, the applesauce, chutney and raisins to boiling, stirring occasionally; reduce heat. Simmer uncovered 3 minutes. Serve with duckling.

8 servings.

Cooking with American Wine

CHAPTER 2

Sea and Stream

Ginger-sauced Fish

2-pound pan-dressed pike or sea bass
2 tablespoons lemon juice
1 tablespoon vegetable oil
2 teaspoons finely chopped gingerroot
1/2 teaspoon salt
2 green onions (with tops)
Ginger Sauce (below)

Remove head from fish. Slash fish crosswise 3 times on each side. Mix lemon juice, oil, gingerroot and salt; brush in cavity and on outside of fish. Cover and refrigerate 1 hour.

Place fish on rack over water in steamer or roasting pan (water should not touch rack; if necessary, elevate rack by placing on custard cups). Cover tightly and heat to boiling; reduce heat. Steam over simmering water until fish flakes easily with fork, about 20 minutes. (Add more boiling water if necessary).

Cut green onions into 2-inch pieces; cut pieces into thin strips. Prepare Ginger Sauce. Carefully remove skin from hot fish and discard; place fish on warm platter. Pour half of the Ginger Sauce over fish; sprinkle with green onions. Serve with remaining Ginger Sauce.

6 servings.

GINGER SAUCE

1 tablespoon finely chopped gingerroot
1 teaspoon finely chopped garlic
2 tablespoons vegetable oil
1/2 cup Pinot Blanc or dry white wine
1/4 cup soy sauce
1/4 cup chili sauce
1/2 teaspoon sugar
4 to 6 drops red pepper sauce
1 tablespoon cornstarch
2 tablespoons cold water

Cook and stir gingerroot and garlic in oil in 1-quart saucepan until light brown. Stir in remaining ingredients except cornstarch and water. Heat to boiling; reduce heat. Cover and simmer 10 minutes. Mix cornstarch and cold water; stir into ginger mixture. Heat to boiling; boil and stir 1 minute.

*P*an-dressed fish are ready to cook—scaled and eviscerated, usually with the tail and fins removed. The head can either be removed or remain, depending on personal preference. Each pound of pan-dressed fish will yield about 8 ounces of fillet, so plan your purchases accordingly.

Trout with Cabbage and Apples

5 cups coarsely shredded cabbage (about ½ large head)
¾ cup Gewürztraminer or dry white wine
¼ teaspoon salt
¼ teaspoon caraway seed
2 green onions (with tops), thinly sliced
2 medium unpared tart cooking apples, coarsely chopped
4 pan-dressed rainbow trout or whitefish (8 to 10 ounces each)
Vegetable oil

Heat oven to 400°. Heat cabbage, wine, salt, caraway seed and green onions to boiling in 3-quart saucepan; reduce heat. Simmer uncovered, stirring frequently, just until cabbage is limp, about 1 minute. Stir in apples.

Place mixture in ungreased rectangular baking dish, 13 × 9 × 2 inches. Arrange fish on top; brush fish with oil. Bake uncovered until fish flakes easily with fork, about 25 minutes. Garnish with apple slices if desired.

4 servings.

Halibut with Basil Sauce

4 small halibut steaks, 1 inch thick (about 1½ pounds)
2 cups Chardonnay or dry white wine
2 tablespoons snipped fresh basil leaves or ½ teaspoon dried basil
  leaves
¼ teaspoon salt
1 green onion (with top), thinly sliced
1 package (16 ounces) frozen French-style green beans
½ cup whipping cream
2 tablespoons margarine or butter

Heat halibut steaks, wine, basil, salt and green onion to boiling in 10-inch skillet; reduce heat. Simmer uncovered until fish flakes easily with fork, 12 to 15 minutes.

Cook green beans as directed on package; drain. Arrange green beans on serving platter. Carefully remove fish from skillet, using slotted spatula. Remove skin and discard. Place fish on top of green beans; keep warm.

Heat wine mixture in skillet to boiling. Boil 5 minutes. Stir in whipping cream and margarine. Heat to boiling, stirring constantly. Boil and stir until slightly thickened, about 5 minutes. Serve sauce with fish. Garnish with fresh basil if desired.

4 servings.

Caraway is a small, almost black, crescent-shaped seed that has been used as a breath freshener and as a digestive aid. It's a spice that enjoys wide popularity, flavoring everything from cheeses, sausages and breads to liquors and liqueurs. Sauerkraut and other traditional German cabbage dishes rarely lack caraway.

Trout with Cabbage and Apples

Cooking with American Wine

Glazed Salmon

Green Mayonnaise (right)
1½ cups Chenin Blanc or dry white wine, plus additional wine as
    needed for poaching
1 cup water
1 small onion, sliced
1 stalk celery (with leaves), cut up
4 sprigs parsley
5 black peppercorns
1 bay leaf
½ teaspoon salt
¼ teaspoon dried thyme leaves
¼ teaspoon dried tarragon leaves
8 salmon steaks, 1 inch thick (about 4 pounds)
1 envelope unflavored gelatin
2 cups Chenin Blanc or dry white wine
Pitted ripe olives
Pimiento
Green onion tops

Prepare Green Mayonnaise. Heat 1½ cups wine, the water, onion, celery, parsley, peppercorns, bay leaf, salt, thyme and tarragon to boiling in 10-inch skillet; reduce heat. Cover and simmer 5 to 10 minutes.

Place 4 of the salmon steaks in wine mixture. Add just enough water to cover steaks. Heat to boiling; reduce heat. Simmer uncovered until fish flakes easily with fork, 12 to 15 minutes. Remove fish, using slotted spatula; drain on wire rack. Remove skin and discard. Repeat with remaining salmon steaks, adding equal parts wine and water to cover fish. Place wire rack of fish in shallow pan. Cover and refrigerate until cold.

Sprinkle gelatin on ½ cup of the wine in small bowl. Place bowl in pan of hot water over low heat until gelatin is dissolved, about 5 minutes. Stir in the remaining 1½ cups wine. Place bowl in pan of ice and water and stir occasionally until mixture begins to thicken, 20 to 25 minutes. (Mixture should be consistency of unbeaten egg white.)

For flower decorations, cut olives lengthwise into fourths. Cut circles from pimiento; use green onion tops for stems. Spoon two-thirds of the gelatin mixture over cold fish until steaks are completely coated. Arrange decorations on top; spoon remaining gelatin mixture over decorations. (If mixture thickens, set bowl in pan of hot water.) Refrigerate until gelatin is firm. Serve with Green Mayonnaise.

8 servings.

Cold salmon is perfect for summertime luncheons. A prettily arranged plate of peachy-pink salmon served with fresh-tasting Green Mayonnaise is always impressive. The decorations set in aspic are typical of salmon presentation at its most formal yet are not difficult to make.

GREEN MAYONNAISE

2 cups mayonnaise or salad dressing
½ cup finely chopped fresh spinach
½ cup snipped parsley
1 tablespoon snipped chives
1 tablespoon tarragon vinegar
2 to 3 teaspoons snipped fresh dill weed or 1 teaspoon dried dill
    weed

Place all ingredients in blender container. Cover and blend on high speed until smooth. Refrigerate at least 2 hours.

Salmon with Champagne Sauce

3 cups water
2 teaspoons snipped fresh thyme leaves or ½ teaspoon dried thyme
    leaves
½ teaspoon salt
4 salmon steaks, 1 inch thick (about 2 pounds)
Champagne Sauce (below)

Heat water, thyme and salt to boiling in 10-inch skillet. Add salmon steaks. Heat to boiling; reduce heat. Cover and simmer until fish flakes easily with fork, 10 to 12 minutes.

Prepare Champagne Sauce. Carefully remove fish, using slotted spatula. Arrange fish on warm platter. Spoon about half of the Champagne Sauce over fish. Serve with remaining sauce.

4 servings.

CHAMPAGNE SAUCE

½ cup Champagne
¼ cup whipping cream
½ teaspoon snipped fresh thyme leaves or ¼ teaspoon dried thyme
    leaves
2 egg yolks, beaten

Mix together Champagne, whipping cream and thyme in 1-quart saucepan. Cook over medium heat, stirring constantly, just until hot (do not boil). Stir half of the hot mixture gradually into egg yolks; stir yolks into hot mixture in saucepan. Heat to boiling, stirring constantly. Boil and stir 1 minute.

A generous supply of flavorful olive oil should be a staple. (The ancient Greeks would have agreed; they used it for cooking, preserving, dressing vegetables and annointing their skin—even for fueling their lamps.) The various types of oil available can be confusing. "Extra virgin" and "virgin" olive oils come from the first cold pressing of the olives. Then, from these already-crushed olives, "pure" olive oil can be extracted with the addition of chemicals and heat. Extra virgin is the best quality and by law must have less than 1 percent acidity. Virgin is more acidic but can be quite delicious. A good rule of thumb: the deeper green the color of the oil, the more pronounced the olive flavor.

Cilantro is also known as "Mexican" or "Chinese" parsley, depending on the orientation of the recipe that calls for it. The bright green leaves are aromatic with a distinctive pungency that gives this fish its south-of-the-border flavor. Sprigs of cilantro make a delicious garnish.

Baked Fish with Tomato Sauce

¼ cup olive oil
½ cup dry bread crumbs
2 pounds red snapper, cod or haddock fillets
¼ teaspoon salt
¼ cup lemon juice
1 cup snipped parsley
½ cup olive oil
½ cup Johannisberg Riesling or dry white wine
¼ cup tomato sauce
¼ teaspoon salt
¼ teaspoon pepper
2 cloves garlic, finely chopped
½ cup dry bread crumbs

Heat oven to 350°. Pour ¼ cup oil evenly in a rectangular baking dish, 13 × 9 × 2 inches. Sprinkle ½ cup bread crumbs over oil. Place fish in single layer in baking dish; sprinkle with ¼ teaspoon salt. Pour lemon juice on fish.

Mix remaining ingredients except ½ cup bread crumbs; spoon over fish. Sprinkle with bread crumbs. Bake uncovered until fish flakes easily with fork, about 40 minutes. Remove fish to warm platter.

6 servings.

Salsa Fish

1 pound fish fillets (¼ to ½ inch thick)
2 tablespoons margarine or butter
1 medium tomato, chopped
1 small green bell pepper, chopped
1 small onion, chopped
2 tablespoons finely snipped cilantro or parsley
¼ teaspoon salt
¼ cup Gewürztraminer or dry white wine

If fish fillets are large, cut into 4 serving pieces. Heat margarine in 10-inch skillet over medium heat until melted. Arrange fish in single layer in skillet. Cook uncovered, turning once, until fish flakes easily with a fork, 4 to 6 minutes. Remove fish to warm platter; keep warm.

Cook remaining ingredients except wine in skillet over medium heat, stirring frequently, until bell pepper and onion are crisp-tender, 3 to 5 minutes. Stir in wine. Heat until hot. Spoon mixture over fish.

4 servings.

Cooking with American Wine

Baked Flounder with Mushrooms

1 pound flounder fillets
½ teaspoon paprika
¼ teaspoon salt
⅛ teaspoon pepper
⅓ cup sliced leeks (with green tops)
4 ounces mushrooms, sliced (about 1½ cups), or 1 can (4 ounces)
    mushroom stems and pieces, drained
2 tablespoons margarine or butter
½ cup Sémillon or dry white wine
¼ cup sliced almonds
3 tablespoons grated Parmesan cheese

Heat oven to 375°. If flounder fillets are large, cut into 4 serving pieces. Arrange in ungreased square baking dish, 8 × 8 × 2 inches; sprinkle with paprika, salt and pepper. Cook and stir leeks and mushrooms in margarine until leeks are tender; stir in wine. Pour mushroom mixture over fish; sprinkle with almonds and Parmesan cheese. Bake uncovered until fish flakes with fork, about 25 minutes.

4 servings.

This flounder is simplicity itself, a family dish ideal for those "hurry-up" evenings. Serve with hot, fluffy rice in order to savor all of the subtle sauce.

Tropical Kabobs

1 pound cod fillets, cut into 1-inch pieces
½ cup Tropical-flavored Wine Cooler, French Colombard or dry
    white wine
1 tablespoon vegetable oil
1 tablespoon snipped fresh rosemary leaves or 1 teaspoon dried
    rosemary leaves, crushed
½ teaspoon salt
1 bay leaf, crushed
1 can (8¼ ounces) pineapple chunks, drained
4 apricots, cut into fourths

Place cod fillet pieces in shallow glass dish or plastic bag. Mix wine cooler, oil, rosemary, salt and bay leaf; pour over fish. Cover and refrigerate at least 1 hour.

Drain fish, reserving wine cooler mixture. Alternate fish chunks, pineapple chunks and apricot pieces on each of eight 8- to 10-inch metal skewers, leaving space between each. Cover and grill kabobs 5 to 6 inches from medium coals, turning and brushing 2 or 3 times with reserved wine cooler mixture, until fish flakes easily with fork, 10 to 15 minutes. Serve with hot cooked rice if desired.

4 servings.

Fish Fillets with Mushrooms

2 pounds fish fillets
8 ounces mushrooms, sliced (about 3 cups)
2 green onions (with tops), finely chopped
2 tablespoons margarine or butter
¾ cup Grey Riesling or dry white wine
1 tablespoon lemon juice
2 tablespoons margarine or butter
2 tablespoons all-purpose flour
½ cup whipping cream
½ teaspoon salt
¼ teaspoon white pepper
¼ cup shredded Swiss cheese (1 ounce)

If fish fillets are large, cut into 8 serving pieces. Cook and stir mushrooms and green onions in 2 tablespoons margarine in 10-inch skillet until mushrooms are tender, about 3 minutes; remove mixture from skillet. Place fish in skillet; add wine, lemon juice and just enough water to cover fish. Heat to boiling; reduce heat. Cover and simmer until fish flakes easily with fork, 4 to 5 minutes. Remove fish to heatproof platter, using slotted spatula; keep warm.

Heat liquid in skillet to boiling; boil until reduced to 1 cup, 7 to 8 minutes. Pour liquid into 1-cup measure; reserve.

Heat 2 tablespoons margarine in skillet until melted; stir in flour. Cook and stir 1 minute; remove from heat. Stir in reserved liquid and the whipping cream. Heat to boiling, stirring constantly. Boil and stir 1 minute. Stir in reserved mushroom mixture, salt and white pepper.

Drain excess liquid from fish. Spoon sauce over fish; sprinkle with cheese. Set oven to broil. Broil with tops 2 to 3 inches from heat until cheese is melted, 2 to 3 minutes.

8 servings.

Vegetable-Sole Roll-ups

½ teaspoon salt
½ teaspoon dried dill weed
¼ teaspoon pepper
6 sole fillets (about 2 pounds)
24 carrot strips, each about 3 × ¼ inch (about 2 medium carrots)
18 green bell pepper strips, each about 3 × ¼ inch (about 1 medium green bell pepper)
¼ cup Chenin Blanc or dry white wine

2 tablespoons margarine or butter
2 tablespoons all-purpose flour
¼ teaspoon salt
⅛ teaspoon pepper
1 cup milk
¼ cup Chenin Blanc or dry white wine

Heat oven to 350°. Mix ½ teaspoon salt, the dill weed and ¼ teaspoon pepper; sprinkle over sole fillets. Place 4 carrot strips and 3 bell pepper strips across one end of each fillet; roll the fillets around the vegetable bundles. Place roll-ups, seam sides down, in ungreased rectangular baking dish, 13 × 9 × 2 inches. Pour ¼ cup wine over fish. Cover with aluminum foil and bake until fish flakes easily with fork, about 40 minutes.

Heat margarine in 1½-quart saucepan until melted; stir in flour and remaining salt and pepper. Cook and stir 1 minute; remove from heat. Stir in milk. Heat to boiling, stirring constantly. Stir in ¼ cup wine. Boil and stir 1 minute.

Arrange fish on warm platter; pour sauce over fish. Garnish with fresh dill weed if desired.

6 servings.

Macadamia-Coconut Fillets

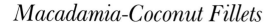

1 pound cod, haddock or mahimahi fillets
2 tablespoons margarine or butter, melted
¼ teaspoon salt
Dash of pepper
2 tablespoons margarine or butter
⅓ cup Gewürztraminer or dry white wine
2 teaspoons cornstarch
¼ cup finely chopped macadamia nuts, toasted
¼ cup flaked coconut, toasted

If fish fillets are large, cut into 4 serving pieces. Mix melted margarine, the salt and pepper; brush on both sides of fish. Set oven control to broil. Place fish on rack in broiler pan. Broil with tops about 4 inches from heat until fish flakes easily with fork, about 8 minutes.

Heat 2 tablespoons margarine in 1-quart saucepan over medium heat until melted. Mix wine and cornstarch; gradually stir into margarine. Heat to boiling, stirring constantly. Boil and stir 1 minute. Arrange fish on warm platter; pour sauce over fish. Top with nuts and coconut.

4 servings.

*T*o toast nuts or coconut, place in a shallow layer in a baking pan. Toast in a 350° oven, stirring frequently, until golden brown, about 5 minutes. If you prefer to microwave, place in a glass pie plate and cook on high (100%) 1½ minutes for ½ cup nuts or coconut, stirring every 30 seconds.

Pompano in Parchment

2 cups water
½ cup Chenin Blanc or dry white wine
½ teaspoon salt
1 medium onion, sliced
3 slices lemon
3 sprigs parsley
1 bay leaf
4 black peppercorns
4 pompano, trout or pike fillets (about 1 pound)
Mushroom Sauce (below)
4 pieces kitchen parchment paper or aluminum foil, 12 × 15
   inches
Vegetable oil
12 cleaned medium uncooked shrimp (about 1 cup)

Heat water, wine, salt, onion, lemon, parsley, bay leaf and peppercorns to boiling in 12-inch skillet; reduce heat. Cover and simmer 5 minutes.

Place fish fillets in skillet. Heat to boiling; reduce heat. Simmer uncovered until fish flakes easily with fork, 3 to 6 minutes. Carefully remove fish using slotted spoon; drain on wire rack. Reserve liquid in skillet for Mushroom Sauce.

Heat oven to 400°. Prepare Mushroom Sauce. Cut each piece of parchment paper into heart shape, about 14 inches wide by 12 inches long. Brush oil over each heart to within ½ inch of edges.

Spoon ¼ cup Mushroom Sauce on one side of each heart. Place 1 piece of fish on sauce. Arrange 3 shrimp on each piece of fish; spoon about 1 tablespoon sauce over shrimp. Fold other half of heart over top. Beginning at top of heart, seal edges by turning up and folding together; twist tip of heart to hold packet closed.

Bake on ungreased cookie sheet until paper puffs up and is light brown, about 15 minutes. To serve, cut a large X on top of each packet; fold back corners.

4 servings.

MUSHROOM SAUCE

Reserved cooking liquid
1 cup sliced mushrooms
3 tablespoons margarine or butter
3 tablespoons all-purpose flour
¼ teaspoon salt

*P*ompano is a delicate-flavored white-fleshed fish found in the warm waters of the Gulf of Mexico. When serving this Creole classic, it's customary to slash open the parchment packets in front of guests so they can savor the aroma (and drama).

1/8 teaspoon white pepper
1/4 cup half-and-half

Strain cooking liquid. Heat to boiling; boil until liquid measures 1 cup; reserve. Cook mushrooms and margarine in 1½-quart saucepan over low heat, stirring occasionally, until mushrooms are tender, about 5 minutes. Stir in flour, salt and white pepper. Cook over low heat, stirring constantly, until bubbly; remove from heat. Gradually stir in reserved liquid and half-and-half. Heat to boiling, stirring constantly. Boil and stir 1 minute.

Creamy Fish Soup with Garlic Toast

1½ cups mayonnaise or salad dressing
3 cloves garlic, finely chopped
1/4 cup margarine or butter
8 slices French bread
1 clove garlic, cut into halves
1 pound fish fillets, cut into 1-inch pieces
1½ cups Chardonnay or dry white wine
1/4 teaspoon salt
6 slices onion
3 slices lemon
5 sprigs parsley
1 bay leaf

Mix mayonnaise and chopped garlic; cover and refrigerate. Heat 2 tablespoons of the margarine in 10-inch skillet over medium heat until melted. Cook 4 of the bread slices in margarine, turning once, until brown; rub one side of toasted bread with half-clove garlic. Repeat with remaining margarine and bread.

Place fish fillet pieces in same skillet. Add remaining ingredients; if necessary, add just enough water to cover fish. Heat to boiling; reduce heat. Simmer uncovered until fish flakes easily with fork, about 6 minutes. Remove fish, using slotted spoon; keep warm.

Strain cooking liquid; return to skillet. Gradually beat in mayonnaise mixture, using wire whisk or spoon. Cook over low heat, stirring constantly, until hot and slightly thickened. Fold in fish. Place 2 slices garlic toast upright in each of 4 soup bowls. Pour soup between slices; sprinkle with paprika if desired.

4 servings.

California Fish Stew

1 cup sliced celery
1 small onion, thinly sliced
2 cloves garlic, crushed
1 tablespoon olive or vegetable oil
1/4 cup snipped parsley
1 cup Pinot Blanc or dry white wine
1 tablespoon snipped fresh basil leaves or 1 teaspoon dried basil
  leaves
1 tablespoon snipped fresh oregano leaves or 1 teaspoon dried
  oregano leaves
1/2 teaspoon salt
1/4 teaspoon pepper
2 large tomatoes or 4 plum tomatoes, seeded and coarsely chopped
1 can (14 1/2 ounces) chicken broth
1 package (9 ounces) frozen artichoke hearts
1 pound fish fillets, cut into 2-inch pieces

Cook and stir celery, onion and garlic in oil in 4-quart Dutch oven over medium heat until onion is tender. Stir in remaining ingredients except fish. Heat to boiling; reduce heat. Cover and simmer 10 minutes; add fish. Cover and simmer until fish flakes easily with fork, about 10 minutes.

4 to 6 servings.

Clam Chowder

2 cans (6 1/2 ounces each) minced clams
3 slices bacon, cut into 1/2-inch pieces
1 medium onion, chopped
1 cup fresh or frozen whole kernel corn
3/4 cup Chardonnay or dry white wine
1/8 teaspoon pepper
1 medium unpeeled potato, cut into cubes
1 cup whipping cream
1 tablespoon snipped parsley

Drain clams, reserving 1/2 cup liquid. Cook bacon in 2-quart saucepan over medium heat, stirring frequently, until almost brown. Stir in onion, and continue cooking until bacon is crisp. Stir in corn, wine, pepper, potato, clams and reserved liquid. Heat to boiling; reduce heat. Cover and simmer until potato is tender, about 15 minutes. Stir in whipping cream. Heat, stirring occasionally, just until hot (do not boil). Stir in parsley.

4 servings.

*F*ish is leaner than the leanest meat. Even so, there are fat and lean fish. The flesh of fat fish (salmon, eel, mackerel and white fish, for example) contains enough oil so that the fish bakes or broils nicely, without drying out. The lean fish (pike, cod, red snapper and swordfish) sometimes require the addition of a little fat to stay moist.

California Fish Stew

Manhattan Clam Linguine

3 quarts water
1 teaspoon salt
2 cans (6½ ounces each) minced clams, drained (reserve liquid)
1 package (8 ounces) linguine or spaghetti
¼ cup margarine or butter
2 tablespoons snipped parsley
1 tablespoon snipped fresh basil leaves or 1½ teaspoons dried
* basil leaves*
¾ teaspoon snipped fresh thyme leaves or ¼ teaspoon dried thyme
* leaves*
Dash of pepper
3 cloves garlic, finely chopped
½ cup whipping cream
¼ cup Emerald Riesling or dry white wine
¼ cup grated Parmesan cheese

Heat water, salt and reserved clam liquid to boiling in 4-quart Dutch oven. Gradually add linguine. Boil uncovered, stirring occasionally, just until tender, 8 to 10 minutes; drain. Return to Dutch oven; toss with 2 tablespoons of the margarine.

Heat remaining 2 tablespoons margarine in 2-quart saucepan. Stir in parsley, basil, thyme, pepper, garlic and clams. Cook over low heat, stirring constantly, until clams are heated through. Stir in whipping cream and wine; heat through, stirring occasionally. Pour over linguine; add Parmesan cheese. Toss until evenly coated.

4 servings.

Manhattan Clam Linguine

Marinated Butterflied Shrimp

1 pound fresh large uncooked shrimp (18 to 20 in shells)
½ cup Johannisberg Riesling or dry white wine
1 tablespoon snipped parsley
1 tablespoon vegetable oil
1 tablespoon snipped fresh basil leaves or 1 teaspoon dried basil
  leaves
¼ teaspoon salt
1 bay leaf, crushed
½ lemon, thinly sliced

Peel shrimp. Make a deep cut lengthwise down back of each shrimp; wash out sand vein. Press each shrimp flat into butterfly shape. Place shrimp in shallow glass dish or plastic bag. Mix remaining ingredients except lemon slices; pour over shrimp. Cover tightly and refrigerate at least 1 hour.

Arrange shrimp in lightly greased hinged wire grill basket; reserve wine mixture. Cover and grill about 4 inches from medium coals, turning basket and brushing shrimp 2 or 3 times with wine mixture until shrimp are pink, 6 to 10 minutes. Garnish with lemon slices and, if desired, parsley.

4 servings.

BROILED MARINATED BUTTERFLIED SHRIMP: Prepare as directed above, except set oven control to broil. Arrange shrimp on lightly greased rack in broiler pan; reserve wine mixture. Broil with tops about 4 inches from heat, turning and brushing once with wine mixture, until shrimp are pink, about 4 minutes each side.

Marinated Butterflied Shrimp

Cooking with American Wine

Shrimp Kabobs

1 pound fresh large uncooked shrimp (18 to 20 in shells) or
* frozen shrimp, thawed*
1/2 cup Sauvignon Blanc or dry white wine
1/4 teaspoon salt
1/4 teaspoon ground nutmeg
1/8 teaspoon pepper
12 whole medium mushrooms
1 small, unpared eating apple, cut into 1-inch pieces
4 cherry tomatoes
1/4 cup margarine or butter
Hot cooked rice

Peel shrimp. Make a shallow cut lengthwise down back of each shrimp; wash out sand vein. Place shrimp, wine, salt, nutmeg and pepper in plastic bag. Close bag tightly; place in pan and refrigerate 2 hours, turning occasionally.

Remove shrimp, reserving wine mixture. Alternate shrimp, mushrooms and apple pieces on each of 4 metal skewers, leaving space between each. Place cherry tomato on end of each skewer.

Set oven control to broil. Place kabobs on rack in broiler pan. Heat reserved wine mixture and margarine until margarine is melted. Brush kabobs with wine-margarine mixture. Broil with tops about 4 inches from heat, turning and brushing once with wine-margarine mixture, until shrimp are pink, about 5 minutes. Place kabobs on rice. Drizzle with remaining wine-margarine mixture.

4 servings.

*W*hether big, fresh shrimp have come your way or frozen shrimp are tucked in the freezer, Shrimp Kabobs will make the most of them. Serve with a salad of assorted greens and homemade rolls.

Baked Shrimp with Cheese

6 eggs
2 1/2 cups milk
1/2 cup Grey Riesling or dry white wine
2 tablespoons snipped parsley
3/4 teaspoon dry mustard
1/4 teaspoon salt
2 cups shredded process sharp American cheese (8 ounces)
10 slices white bread (crusts removed), cut into 1/4-inch cubes
2 cans (4 1/2 ounces each) small shrimp, drained

Heat oven to 325°. Beat eggs, milk, wine, parsley, mustard and salt, using hand beater. Stir in remaining ingredients. Pour into ungreased rectangular baking dish, 12 × 7½ × 2 inches. Bake uncovered until center is set, about 1 hour.

8 servings.

Scallops with Shrimp and Artichokes

12 ounces fresh scallops or 1 package (12 ounces) frozen scallops, thawed
4 ounces mushrooms, sliced (about 1½ cups)
1 small red or green bell pepper, chopped
¼ cup margarine or butter
2 tablespoons all-purpose flour
¼ teaspoon salt
1 cup half-and-half
½ cup Grey Riesling or dry white wine
1 can (14 ounces) artichoke hearts, drained and cut into halves
1 package (6 ounces) frozen cooked shrimp, thawed
¼ cup grated Parmesan cheese
2 tablespoons snipped parsley

If scallops are large, cut into 1-inch pieces. Place scallops in 2-quart saucepan; add just enough water to cover. Heat to boiling; reduce heat. Simmer uncovered until scallops turn white, about 5 minutes; drain. Cook and stir mushrooms and bell pepper in margarine over medium heat until tender, about 4 minutes; remove vegetables, using slotted spoon. Stir flour and salt into margarine. Cook, stirring constantly, until smooth and bubbly; remove from heat. Stir in half-and-half. Heat to boiling, stirring constantly. Boil and stir 1 minute; stir in cooked vegetables.

Stir in wine, artichoke hearts, shrimp and scallops. Heat until shrimp and scallops are hot, about 10 minutes. Sprinkle with Parmesan cheese and parsley.

8 servings.

*T*he western world has Catherine de Médicis to thank for the general popularity of the artichoke. What is sold by the greengrocer as an artichoke is really the flower of the artichoke plant. The struggle to prepare these prickly, choke-filled flowers is always rewarded by the delicate, buttery artichoke hearts.

Warm Scallop Salad

1 pound fresh scallops or frozen scallops, thawed
4 ounces mushrooms, sliced (about 1 1/2 cups)
1 small leek (with green top), sliced (about 1/3 cup)
2 tablespoons margarine or butter
2 tablespoons olive or vegetable oil
1/2 cup Sémillon or dry white wine
1/8 teaspoon dried tarragon leaves
2 tablespoons cold water
2 teaspoons cornstarch
3 cups shredded assorted greens
1 lemon, cut into wedges

If scallops are large, cut into 1-inch pieces. Cook and stir mushrooms and leek in margarine and oil in 10-inch skillet 5 minutes. Stir in wine and tarragon. Heat to boiling. Add scallops; reduce heat. Simmer uncovered, stirring occasionally, until scallops turn white, 3 to 4 minutes. Mix water and cornstarch; stir into scallop mixture. Heat to boiling. Boil and stir 1 minute. Spoon scallop mixture over greens; garnish with lemon wedges.

4 servings.

Scallops in Cream Sauce

1½ pounds fresh scallops or 2 packages (12 ounces each) frozen
   scallops, thawed
1 cup Pinot Blanc or dry white wine
¼ cup snipped parsley
½ teaspoon salt
4 ounces mushrooms, sliced (about 1½ cups)
2 shallots or green onions, chopped
5 tablespoons margarine or butter
3 tablespoons all-purpose flour
½ cup half-and-half
½ cup shredded Swiss cheese (2 ounces)
1 cup soft bread crumbs (about 1½ slices bread)
2 tablespoons margarine or butter, melted
Margarine or butter, melted

If scallops are large, cut into 1-inch pieces. Place scallops, wine, parsley and salt in 3-quart saucepan. Add just enough water to cover scallops. Heat to boiling; reduce heat. Simmer uncovered until scallops turn white, about 8 minutes. Remove scallops, using slotted spoon. Heat liquid to boiling. Boil until reduced to 1 cup; strain and reserve liquid.

Cook and stir mushrooms and shallots in 2 tablespoons margarine in 3-quart saucepan until shallots are tender, 5 to 6 minutes. Remove from pan. Add 3 tablespoons margarine; heat until melted. Remove from heat; stir in flour. Cook over low heat, stirring constantly, until smooth and bubbly. Remove from heat; stir in reserved cooking liquid. Cook and stir 1 minute. Stir in half-and-half, scallops, mushrooms, shallots and ¼ cup of the cheese; heat.

Toss bread crumbs in 2 tablespoons melted margarine. Brush 5 baking shells or 4½-ounce ramekins with melted margarine. Divide scallop mixture among baking shells. Sprinkle with remaining cheese and the bread crumbs. Set oven control to broil. Broil with tops about 5 inches from heat, until crumbs are light brown, 3 to 5 minutes.

5 servings.

*B*eautiful scallop shells have been celebrated by artists for centuries. It isn't absolutely necessary to serve this variation of *Coquilles Saint Jacques* in baking shells, but it is a lovely presentation. The ivory sauce gets a sprinkling of buttery crumbs and a gilding under the broiler.

Crab in Puff Pastry

½ package (17½-ounce size) frozen puff pastry
2 tablespoons thinly sliced green onion (with top)
2 tablespoons margarine or butter
2 tablespoons all-purpose flour
½ cup milk
½ cup whipping cream
1½ cups cooked crabmeat, lobster or shrimp
½ cup Sauvignon Blanc or dry white wine
2 tablespoons snipped parsley
1 teaspoon finely shredded lemon peel
¼ teaspoon salt
⅛ teaspoon pepper

Thaw 1 sheet of puff pastry as directed on package. Heat oven to 350°. Unfold pastry and place on lightly floured surface. Roll into 10-inch square. Cut into halves; place one piece on top of another. Roll to seal edges; cut crosswise into 4 equal pieces. Bake until golden brown, about 20 minutes.

Cook onion in margarine in 2-quart saucepan over low heat until tender. Stir in flour. Cook over low heat, stirring constantly, until mixture is bubbly; remove from heat.

Gradually stir in milk and whipping cream. Heat to boiling, stirring constantly. Boil and stir 1 minute. Stir in remaining ingredients; heat through.

Split each warm pastry horizontally with fork. Spoon crab mixture over bottom halves; top with remaining pastry halves. Garnish with parsley if desired.

4 servings.

*N*ow, good quality puff pastry can be bought frozen, making it easy to transform any common, saucy dish into a memorable event. If you like, substitute imitation crab for the real thing here. It is sometimes sold under the name *surimi* and is made from processed, firm-fleshed white fish. In sauces, *surimi* can have a texture and flavor surprisingly like that of crabmeat.

CHAPTER 3

Meaty Mainstays

Beef Roast with Winter Fruit

1 cup water
½ cup dried apricots, cut into halves
½ cup pitted prunes, cut into halves
1 teaspoon salt
½ teaspoon ground ginger
¼ teaspoon pepper
4- to 5-pound beef arm, blade or cross-rib pot roast
1 tablespoon vegetable oil
1½ cups chopped onion
½ cup Zinfandel or dry red wine
2 cloves garlic, finely chopped
1 can (6 ounces) pitted olives, drained
2 cups sliced mushrooms (about 5 ounces)

Pour water over apricots and prunes; reserve. Mix salt, ginger and pepper; rub over roast. Heat oil in 4-quart Dutch oven. Cook beef in hot oil until brown on all sides; drain. Add onion, wine and garlic. Heat to boiling; reduce heat. Cover tightly and simmer on top of range or in 325° oven 2 hours.

Add apricots and prunes, olives and mushrooms. Cover and cook until beef is tender, about 1 hour longer.

12 servings.

Marinated Beef Roast with Potato Dumplings

1½ cups cold water
1 cup Cabernet Sauvignon or dry red wine
½ cup red wine vinegar
1 large onion, thinly sliced
5 black peppercorns, crushed
4 whole juniper berries, crushed
1 large bay leaf
3- to 4-pound beef rolled rump roast
3 tablespoons vegetable oil
½ cup water
Potato Dumplings (right)
12 gingersnaps, crushed (about ½ cup)

Heat 1½ cups water, the wine, vinegar, onion, peppercorns, juniper berries and bay leaf to boiling. Remove from heat; cool to room temperature.

Prick beef roast in several places, using fork. Place roast in large glass bowl; pour wine mixture over beef. Cover tightly and refrigerate 2 to 3 days, turning roast several times each day.

Remove beef from wine mixture; pat dry. Strain wine mixture, reserving liquid and discarding onion and spices. Cook beef in oil in 4-quart Dutch oven, turning occasionally, until brown on all sides, about 10 minutes. Remove beef; pour fat from Dutch oven.

Heat 2 cups of the reserved wine mixture and ½ cup water to boiling in Dutch oven (reserve remaining wine mixture). Return beef to Dutch oven; reduce heat. Cover and simmer until beef is tender, about 2 hours.

Prepare Potato Dumplings. Remove beef to warm platter; keep warm. Pour liquid from Dutch oven into 4-cup measure; skim off fat. Add enough reserved wine mixture to liquid to measure 2½ cups if necessary. (If liquid measures more than 2½ cups, boil rapidly to reduce amount to 2½ cups.) Return to Dutch oven. Stir in gingersnaps. Heat over medium heat, stirring frequently, 10 minutes; strain. Serve sauce with beef and Potato Dumplings.

8 servings.

*T*he flavor of the juniper berry, that hard, bluish purple fruit of the evergreen juniper bush, is commonly associated with Dutch gin (*genever*). These spicy berries also add zip to stewed rabbit or beef, fried pork or roast game, as well as to classic red cabbage dishes.

POTATO DUMPLINGS

2 tablespoons margarine or butter
2 slices white bread (crusts removed), cut into ½-inch cubes
3½ cups riced, cooked potatoes (5 medium)
1 cup all-purpose flour
1½ teaspoons salt
⅛ teaspoon white pepper
⅛ teaspoon ground nutmeg
2 eggs, beaten
4 quarts water
2 teaspoons salt
2 teaspoons margarine or butter
2 tablespoons dry bread crumbs

Heat 2 tablespoons margarine in 8-inch skillet until melted. Cook bread cubes in margarine over medium heat, stirring frequently, until golden brown.

Mix potatoes, flour, 1½ teaspoons salt, the white pepper and nutmeg in medium bowl. Stir in eggs; beat until dough holds its shape. Flour hands lightly. Shape about 2 tablespoons dough into ball. Press hole in center with fingertip; drop 4 bread cubes into hole. Seal dumpling by shaping into ball again. Repeat with remaining dough and bread cubes.

Heat water and 2 teaspoons salt to boiling in 6-quart Dutch oven. Heat 2 teaspoons margarine in skillet until melted. Cook and stir bread crumbs in margarine until margarine is absorbed; reserve.

Drop dumplings into boiling water; stir once or twice; reduce heat. Simmer uncovered until dumplings are done, 12 to 15 minutes. Remove with slotted spoon. Sprinkle with reserved bread crumbs.

Crushed Pepper Beef Kabobs

1½ *pounds beef boneless round, tip or chuck steak*
½ *cup Zinfandel or dry red wine*
1 tablespoon olive or vegetable oil
½ *teaspoon salt*
1 clove garlic, cut into halves
2 tablespoons prepared mustard
2 tablespoons black peppercorns, coarsely crushed
2 small onions, cut lengthwise into fourths
2 small zucchini, cut into 1-inch slices
1 red or yellow bell pepper, cut into 1-inch pieces
4 mushrooms
Olive oil

Trim excess fat from beef steak; cut beef into 1-inch cubes. Place in glass or plastic bowl. Mix wine, 1 tablespoon oil, the salt and garlic; pour over beef. Cover and refrigerate at least 6 hours but no longer than 24 hours, stirring occasionally.

Remove beef; drain thoroughly. Thread beef cubes on four 11-inch metal skewers, leaving space between cubes. Brush with mustard; sprinkle with peppercorns.

Set oven control to broil. Place kabobs on rack in broiler pan. Broil with tops about 3 inches from heat 5 minutes; turn over. Broil 5 minutes longer.

Alternate onion, zucchini, bell pepper, and mushrooms on each of four 11-inch metal skewers, leaving space between each. Place kabobs on rack in broiler pan with beef. Turn beef; brush vegetables with oil. Broil kabobs, turning and brushing vegetables with oil, until beef is done and vegetables are crisp-tender, 5 to 6 minutes.

4 servings.

*T*hese kabobs are not for timid taste buds! With a nod to France, this recipe is a twist on the traditional favorite, *steak au poivre*. For delicious variations try Dijon-style mustard or a mustard flavored with herbs or garlic.

Crushed Pepper Beef Kabobs

Marinated Steak with Mushroom Sauce

1½-pound beef boneless sirloin steak, about 1½ inches thick
½ cup Cabernet Sauvignon or dry red wine
1 tablespoon snipped fresh basil leaves or 1 teaspoon dried basil leaves
¼ teaspoon salt
¼ teaspoon pepper
Mushroom Sauce (below)

Trim excess fat from beef steak. Mix wine, basil, salt and pepper in shallow glass or plastic dish. Place beef in dish, turning once to coat both sides. Cover and refrigerate at least 8 hours but no longer than 24 hours, turning beef occasionally.

Set oven control to broil. Remove beef from wine mixture; reserve wine mixture. Place beef on rack in broiler pan. Broil with top about 4 inches from heat until desired doneness, 10 to 15 minutes on each side for medium. Sprinkle with salt and pepper if desired. Prepare Mushroom Sauce; serve with beef.

6 servings.

MUSHROOM SAUCE

1 tablespoon margarine or butter
1½ cups sliced mushrooms (about 4 ounces)
Reserved wine mixture
⅓ cup water
1 tablespoon cornstarch

Heat margarine in 2-quart saucepan until bubbly. Cook mushrooms in margarine over medium heat, stirring occasionally, until tender, about 4 minutes. Add reserved wine mixture; heat to boiling. Mix water and cornstarch. Stir cornstarch mixture into mushroom mixture. Heat to boiling, stirring constantly. Boil and stir 1 minute.

Chilled Beef Slices with Salsa

1½-pound beef flank steak
¾ cup Zinfandel or dry red wine
1 tablespoon snipped fresh basil leaves or 1 teaspoon dried basil
  leaves
1 tablespoon snipped fresh oregano leaves or 1 teaspoon dried
  oregano leaves
½ teaspoon salt
2 cloves garlic, crushed
1 pound bulk pork sausage
1 small onion, chopped
¼ cup dry bread crumbs
1 can (4 ounces) chopped green chilies, drained
1 medium carrot
3 hard-cooked eggs, peeled
2 tablespoons olive or vegetable oil
1 cup water
1 jar (12 ounces) salsa

Split beef steak lengthwise almost into halves; open and place in shallow glass or plastic dish. Mix wine, basil, oregano, salt and garlic; pour over beef. Cover and refrigerate at least 1 hour.

Drain; reserve wine mixture. Cook and stir sausage and onion in 4-quart Dutch oven over medium heat until sausage is done; drain. Stir in bread crumbs and chilies. Spread sausage mixture on cut side of open beef to within 1 inch of edges. Cut carrot lengthwise into halves; cut each half lengthwise into 3 strips. Arrange carrot strips crosswise on sausage mixture. Place peeled eggs in a row along one narrow edge of steak. Roll up, beginning at end with eggs; tie with string or secure with wooden picks.

Cook beef roll in oil in same Dutch oven over medium heat, turning carefully, until brown on all sides; drain. Add reserved wine mixture and water. Heat to boiling; reduce heat. Cover and simmer until beef is tender, about 1 hour. Remove beef from liquid. Cover and refrigerate beef until cold, at least 6 hours but no longer than 24 hours.

Spread salsa on serving platter or plate. Slice beef roll; arrange on salsa. Serve with additional salsa if desired.

8 servings.

This savory sausage-filled roll of beef may be prepared up to a day in advance—a perfect main course for a summer buffet. Here, salsa is a zesty, hot-weather alternative to pan gravy.

Beef-Vegetable Stew with Barley

1 pound beef stew meat, cut into 1-inch pieces
1 tablespoon vegetable oil
1 cup Petite Sirah or dry red wine
¼ teaspoon pepper
1 teaspoon snipped fresh rosemary leaves or ¼ teaspoon dried
  rosemary leaves, crushed
1 clove garlic, finely chopped
1 can (10½ ounces) condensed beef broth
1 can (14½ ounces) whole tomatoes, undrained
½ cup uncooked barley
1 cup broccoli flowerets
2 carrots, sliced
1 medium onion, cut into wedges
4 ounces medium mushrooms, cut into halves

Cook and stir beef in oil in 4-quart Dutch oven until brown.
Stir in wine, pepper, rosemary, garlic, beef broth and toma-
toes; break up tomatoes. Heat to boiling; reduce heat.
Cover and simmer 1 hour.

Stir in barley; cover and simmer until beef is almost tender,
about 30 minutes longer. Stir in remaining ingredients.
Cover and simmer until vegetables are tender, about 20
minutes.

4 servings.

Beef-Vegetable Stew with Barley

Red Wine Stew

6 slices bacon, cut into 1-inch pieces
2 pounds beef boneless chuck eye, rolled rump or bottom round
    roast, cut into 1-inch cubes
½ cup all-purpose flour
1½ cups Pinot Noir or dry red wine
1¼ teaspoons salt
1 teaspoon instant beef bouillon
1 teaspoon snipped fresh thyme leaves or ½ teaspoon dried thyme
    leaves
¼ teaspoon pepper
1 clove garlic, chopped
1 bay leaf
8 ounces mushrooms, sliced (about 3 cups)
4 medium onions, sliced
2 tablespoons margarine or butter

Cook bacon in 4-quart Dutch oven until crisp. Remove bacon; reserve. Coat beef with flour and shake off excess; cook and stir beef in hot bacon fat until brown. Drain fat from Dutch oven. Add wine and just enough water to cover beef. Stir in salt, bouillon (dry), thyme, pepper, garlic and bay leaf. Heat to boiling; reduce heat. Cover and simmer until beef is tender, about 1½ hours.

Cook and stir mushrooms and onions in margarine over medium heat until onions are tender. Stir mushrooms, onions and bacon into stew. Cover and simmer 10 minutes. Remove bay leaf.

8 servings.

Layered Stew with White Wine

Layered Stew with White Wine is an example of cooking en daube. This method of braising meat in an aromatic stock of wine and herbs predates heat-regulated ovens. Traditionally, en daube dishes were prepared in daubières, earthenware casseroles with lids deep enough to hold smoldering coals, ensuring long, even cooking.

2 pounds beef round steak, 1 inch thick
2 large onions, thinly sliced
1½ cups thinly sliced carrots
1 cup Chardonnay or dry white wine
2 tablespoons olive or vegetable oil
2 teaspoons snipped fresh thyme leaves or ¼ teaspoon dried thyme
    leaves
1 teaspoon salt
¼ teaspoon pepper
2 cloves garlic, finely chopped
1 bay leaf
8 cups water
½ pound bacon, cut into 2-inch pieces
½ cup all-purpose flour

2 cups sliced mushrooms (about 5 ounces)
2 large tomatoes, peeled and chopped

Cut beef steak into 2½-inch pieces. Mix beef, onions, carrots, wine, oil, thyme, salt, pepper, garlic and bay leaf in large glass bowl. Cover and refrigerate at least 6 hours but no longer than 24 hours, stirring occasionally.

Heat oven to 325°. Heat water to boiling in 4-quart Dutch oven. Add bacon; reduce heat. Simmer uncovered 10 minutes; drain, reserving bacon. Remove beef from wine mixture. Strain wine mixture, reserving vegetables and liquid. Coat beef with flour; shake off excess. Layer half of the bacon and reserved vegetables, the mushrooms, tomatoes and beef in Dutch oven. Top with remaining bacon and vegetables.

Add enough water to reserved liquid to measure 1½ cups. Pour over beef and vegetables; heat to boiling. Cover and bake until beef is tender, about 3 hours. Remove bay leaf.

6 servings.

Marinated Blue Cheese Burgers

1 cup Pinot Noir or dry red wine
1½ pounds lean ground beef
½ cup crushed buttery cracker crumbs (about 12 crackers)
¼ cup sliced green onions (with tops)
2 tablespoons crumbled blue cheese (1 ounce)
¼ teaspoon pepper
6 slices bacon

Remove 2 tablespoons wine for patties; reserve remaining wine for marinating. Mix 2 tablespoons wine and the remaining ingredients except bacon and reserved wine. Shape into 6 oval patties, each about 1¼ inches thick.

Wrap 1 slice bacon around each patty and secure with wooden pick. Arrange patties in shallow glass or plastic dish. Pour reserved wine over patties; cover. Refrigerate, turning once, at least 6 hours but no longer than 24 hours.

Set oven control to broil. Remove patties from wine and place on rack in broiler pan. Broil with tops about 3 inches from heat until desired doneness, about 9 minutes on each side for medium. Serve with additional crumbled blue cheese if desired.

6 servings.

These mouth-watering hamburgers are cheese through and through. Serve them up on toasted rye or onion rolls with crisp relishes for an informal but delicious meal.

Meatballs in Wine Sauce

1 pound ground beef
1 small onion, chopped
½ cup dry bread crumbs
¼ cup water chestnuts, finely chopped
¼ cup milk
½ teaspoon salt
½ teaspoon Worcestershire sauce
⅛ teaspoon pepper
1 egg
Wine Sauce (below)

Heat oven to 400°. Mix all ingredients except Wine Sauce. Shape mixture into 1-inch balls; place in ungreased jelly roll pan, 15½ × 10½ × 1 inch. Bake uncovered until done, about 10 minutes. Prepare Wine Sauce; stir meatballs into Wine Sauce. Garnish with parsley if desired.

6 servings.

WINE SAUCE

¼ cup cold water
3 tablespoons cornstarch
½ cup Pinot Noir or dry red wine
1 can (10½ ounces) condensed beef broth
1 clove garlic, crushed

Mix water and cornstarch in 3-quart saucepan; stir in remaining ingredients gradually. Heat to boiling, stirring constantly. Boil and stir 1 minute.

*N*othing could be easier to prepare than these meatballs. Serve them as a main dish or as party food; they are fabulous kept warm in a chafing dish.

Mostaccioli with Beef and Prosciutto Sauce

1 pound ground beef
2 medium onions, sliced
2 cloves garlic, finely chopped
¾ cup Zinfandel or dry red wine
2 teaspoons snipped fresh rosemary leaves or ½ teaspoon dried
  rosemary leaves, crushed
1 teaspoon sugar
¼ teaspoon ground nutmeg
¼ teaspoon pepper
1 can (28 ounces) whole tomatoes, undrained
¼ pound prosciutto or dried beef, cut into thin strips

1 pound uncooked mostaccioli or ziti
Grated Parmesan cheese

Cook and stir ground beef, onions and garlic in 10-inch skillet until beef is brown; drain. Stir in remaining ingredients except mostaccioli and cheese; break up tomatoes. Cover and simmer 15 minutes, stirring occasionally.

Uncover and simmer about 1 hour longer, stirring occasionally. Prepare mostaccioli as directed on package; drain. Serve beef mixture over mostaccioli; sprinkle with cheese.

8 servings.

Spaghetti with Meat Sauce

1½ pounds ground beef
½ cup finely chopped onion
2 cloves garlic, finely chopped
¼ cup olive oil
½ cup chopped green bell pepper
¼ cup snipped parsley
1 tablespoon snipped fresh basil leaves or ¾ teaspoon dried basil
*   leaves*
2 teaspoons snipped fresh oregano leaves or ½ teaspoon dried
*   oregano leaves*
1½ teaspoons salt
½ teaspoon pepper
¼ teaspoon sugar
3 cans (8 ounces each) tomato sauce
1 can (4 ounces) mushroom stems and pieces, undrained
1 cup Zinfandel or dry red wine
1 package (16 ounces) spaghetti
Grated Parmesan cheese

Cook and stir ground beef, onion and garlic in oil in 4-quart Dutch oven until beef is brown; drain. Stir in remaining ingredients except wine, spaghetti and cheese. Heat to boiling; reduce heat. Cover and simmer 1 hour, stirring occasionally.

Stir in wine. Cover and simmer 30 minutes, stirring occasionally. Uncover and simmer 30 minutes longer, stirring occasionally. Prepare spaghetti as directed on package; drain but do not rinse. Pour sauce over hot spaghetti. Serve with cheese.

6 servings.

Chili

2 pounds ground beef
1 cup chopped onion
1 cup chopped green bell pepper
2 cloves garlic, finely chopped
1 cup Zinfandel or dry red wine
¼ cup Worcestershire sauce
1 tablespoon chili powder
1 teaspoon celery seed
1 teaspoon pepper
½ teaspoon ground cumin
2 cans (16 ounces each) whole tomatoes, undrained
3 cans (15½ ounces each) red kidney beans, undrained

*C*hili recipes
vary greatly in different parts of
the country, and there is keen
competition among the various
schools of chili cookery. When
you prepare this version, look
for an authentic Texas red wine
for cooking—and for serving
with dinner. A full-bodied
Texan Cabernet will stand up to
the spices and beans with brio!

Cook and stir ground beef, onion, bell pepper and garlic in 4-quart Dutch oven until beef is brown; drain. Stir in wine and Worcestershire sauce. Heat to boiling; reduce heat. Simmer uncovered 10 minutes, stirring occasionally.

Stir chili powder, celery seed, pepper and cumin into beef mixture. Simmer uncovered 10 minutes, stirring occasionally. Stir in tomatoes, breaking them up. Heat to boiling; reduce heat. Cover and simmer 30 minutes, stirring occasionally.

Stir in kidney beans. Heat to boiling; reduce heat. Cover and simmer 30 minutes. Uncover and simmer 30 minutes longer, stirring occasionally.

8 servings.

Stuffed Veal Rolls

1 pound veal round, arm or blade steak, ½ inch thick
½ teaspoon salt
⅛ teaspoon pepper
¼ cup finely chopped onion
¼ cup snipped parsley
1 tablespoon margarine or butter
4 thin slices fully cooked smoked ham
4 hard-cooked eggs, peeled
2 tablespoons margarine or butter
6 medium carrots, cut into julienne strips
8 small white onions
½ cup Grey Riesling or dry white wine
½ cup water
2 tablespoons water
2 teaspoons cornstarch

Heat oven to 325°. Trim bone and fat from veal steak; cut veal into 4 pieces. Flatten pieces to ¼-inch thickness between plastic wrap or waxed paper, being careful not to tear veal. Sprinkle one side of veal with salt and pepper. Cook and stir onion and parsley in 1 tablespoon margarine over medium heat until onion is tender, about 5 minutes.

Spread a fourth of onion mixture over each piece of veal. Top each with 1 slice of ham and 1 peeled egg. Roll up carefully, beginning at narrow end; tie string around middle and ends of each roll.

Cook veal rolls in 2 tablespoons margarine in 4-quart Dutch oven over medium heat until brown. Add carrots, onions, wine and ½ cup water. Cover and bake until veal is tender, about 1 hour. Remove veal rolls and vegetables to warm platter; remove strings. Cut each roll into halves; keep warm.

Mix 2 tablespoons water and cornstarch; stir into pan liquid. Heat to boiling, stirring constantly. Boil and stir until thickened, about 2 minutes. Serve with veal rolls.

4 servings.

*S*lices of meat or fillets of fish, rolled around a filling, are known in French as *paupiettes* because they look like fat corks. Grey Riesling—despite the name, it's not related to Johannisberg or White Riesling—flavors the braising liquid.

Braised Veal Shanks

4 pounds veal or beef shanks
¼ cup all-purpose flour
3 tablespoons olive or vegetable oil
1 cup water
½ cup Grey Riesling or dry white wine
2 teaspoons snipped fresh basil leaves or ½ teaspoon dried basil
  leaves
1 teaspoon instant beef bouillon
½ teaspoon salt
¼ teaspoon pepper
1 medium onion, chopped
1 medium carrot, chopped
1 stalk celery, chopped
1 clove garlic, chopped
1 bay leaf
Gremolata (below)

Trim excess fat from veal shanks if necessary. Coat veal with flour and shake off excess. Heat oil in 4-quart Dutch oven over medium heat. Cook veal in hot oil until brown on all sides, about 20 minutes; drain. Add remaining ingredients except Gremolata. Heat to boiling; reduce heat. Cover and simmer until veal is tender, 1½ to 2 hours.

Arrange veal and vegetables on warm platter; keep warm. Skim fat from broth, and remove bay leaf; pour broth over veal. Sprinkle with Gremolata. Serve with hot cooked rice or spaghetti if desired.

6 servings.

GREMOLATA

2 tablespoons snipped parsley
1 teaspoon grated lemon peel
1 clove garlic, finely chopped

Mix all ingredients.

*T*he Italians call this Milanese dish *Osso Buco* ("hollow bone") because the marrow is a delicious dividend after the meat has been enjoyed. It is authentically served with *gremolata*, a spicy condiment of garlic, parsley and citrus rind. Invite guests to sprinkle the pretty green mixture over their veal shanks according to taste.

Barbecued Country-style Ribs

1 cup Ruby Port or sweet red wine
½ cup chili sauce
⅓ cup vinegar
¼ cup honey
2 tablespoons soy sauce

1 tablespoon Worcestershire sauce
2 teaspoons dry mustard
1 teaspoon salt
1 teaspoon horseradish
1 teaspoon red pepper sauce
½ teaspoon pepper
½ teaspoon paprika
3 tablespoons vegetable oil
3 pounds pork country-style ribs

Heat all ingredients except oil and pork ribs to boiling, stirring constantly. Remove from heat and reserve sauce. Heat oven to 350°. Heat oil in 4-quart Dutch oven over low heat. Cook half of the ribs in hot oil until brown; remove ribs. Repeat with remaining ribs; drain.

Return ribs to Dutch oven; pour reserved sauce over ribs. Cover and bake 1 hour. Uncover and bake until done, about 30 minutes longer. Remove ribs to warm platter; keep warm. Strain sauce; skim off fat. Pour sauce over ribs.

6 servings.

Country-style ribs, the meatiest of all pork ribs, are a blade cut from the pig. In fact, sometimes these ribs are called "blade-end country spare ribs."

Cranberry Pork Chops with Rosemary

4 pork loin or rib chops, about 1 inch thick
1 tablespoon vegetable oil
1 tablespoon snipped fresh rosemary leaves or 1 teaspoon dried
   rosemary leaves, crushed
½ teaspoon salt
1 medium onion, sliced and separated into rings
1 cup French Colombard or dry white wine
¼ cup packed brown sugar
½ package (12-ounce size) fresh or frozen cranberries (1½ cups)

Cook pork chops in oil in 10-inch skillet over medium heat until brown on both sides, about 20 minutes; drain. Sprinkle with rosemary and salt. Arrange onion on pork; pour wine into skillet. Heat to boiling; reduce heat. Cover and simmer until pork is done, 30 to 45 minutes. Remove pork to warm platter; keep warm.

Heat liquid in skillet to boiling; boil until thickened and reduced by half. Stir in brown sugar and cranberries. Heat to boiling; reduce heat. Cover and boil gently until cranberries pop, about 5 minutes. Serve over pork. Garnish with fresh rosemary if desired.

4 servings.

Peach-glazed Pork Roast

4-pound pork boneless top loin roast
1½ cups Peach-flavored Wine Cooler
1 tablespoon snipped fresh rosemary leaves or 1 teaspoon dried
  rosemary leaves, crushed
1 teaspoon salt
1 teaspoon dry mustard
1 teaspoon finely shredded lemon peel
2 cloves garlic, crushed
½ cup peach preserves
1 tablespoon cold water
1 teaspoon cornstarch

Place pork roast in shallow glass or plastic dish. Mix wine cooler, rosemary, salt, mustard, lemon peel and garlic; pour over pork. Cover and refrigerate, turning occasionally, at least 12 hours

Heat oven to 325°. Place pork, fat side up, on rack in shallow roasting pan. Insert meat thermometer so tip is in center of the thickest part of pork and does not rest in fat. Pour wine cooler mixture over pork. Bake uncovered 1½ hours, spooning pan drippings over pork occasionally.

Spoon peach preserves over pork. Bake until thermometer registers 170°, about 1 hour longer. Remove pork and rack from pan; keep pork warm. Pour pan drippings into 1-quart saucepan; heat to boiling. Mix water and cornstarch; stir into pan drippings. Heat to boiling, stirring constantly. Boil and stir 1 minute. Serve with pork.

12 servings.

*T*he marinade for this juicy roast recalls many of the same flavors to be found in a jar of chutney: garlic, mustard, peach and citrus. It was the eighteenth-century traders who started Americans on their love of this and other Indian spices and condiments.

Here is hospitality in the time-honored fashion of the old South—peaches with the pork, and enough to feed a crowd!

Peach-glazed Pork Roast

Ham with Apples and Pears

¼ cup packed brown sugar
1 tablespoon cornstarch
⅛ teaspoon ground cloves
1 cup White Zinfandel or rosé wine
1 tablespoon prepared mustard
1 fully cooked smoked ham slice, 1 inch thick (about 2 pounds)
2 unpared all-purpose apples, cut crosswise into 1-inch slices
2 unpared pears, cut crosswise into 1-inch slices

Mix brown sugar, cornstarch and cloves in 1-quart sauce-pan. Stir in wine and mustard. Heat to boiling, stirring constantly. Boil and stir 1 minute.

Set oven control to broil. Place ham slice on rack in broiler pan; arrange apples and pears around ham. Broil with top about 3 inches from heat until ham is light brown, about 10 minutes. Turn ham, apples and pears; broil until ham is light brown, about 6 minutes longer. Brush ham, apples and pears with wine sauce during last 2 minutes of broiling. Serve with remaining sauce.

6 servings.

*B*efore kiwifruit were available from coast to coast, they were known in their obscurity as "Chinese gooseberries." The bright green flesh, speckled with tiny black seeds, has a flavor hard to describe; some say it is a combination of watermelon, strawberry and banana. Kiwis are featured in pastries and fruit salads and make for juicy snacks all on their own. Pork is often served with fruit—kiwifruit adds more exotic flair than applesauce ever could!

Ham with Apples and Pears

Pork Chops with Kiwifruit

4 pork loin or rib chops, about ½ inch thick
½ teaspoon salt
½ cup Chenin Blanc or dry white wine
2 tablespoons packed brown sugar
2 tablespoons lime juice
¼ cup cold water
1 teaspoon cornstarch
1 kiwifruit, peeled and sliced

Cook pork chops in 10-inch skillet over medium heat until brown on both sides, about 20 minutes; drain. Sprinkle with salt. Mix wine, brown sugar and lime juice; pour over pork. Heat to boiling; reduce heat. Cover and simmer until pork is done, 20 to 25 minutes. Remove pork to warm platter; keep warm.

Mix water and cornstarch; gradually stir into skillet. Heat to boiling, stirring constantly. Boil and stir 1 minute. Stir in kiwifruit; pour over pork.

4 servings.

Cooking with American Wine

Grilled Pork with Vegetable Sauce

1-pound pork tenderloin, cut diagonally into 8 slices (about 1½ inches thick)
½ cup Cabernet Sauvignon or dry red wine
1 tablespoon vegetable oil
2 cloves garlic, finely chopped
½ teaspoon instant chicken bouillon
⅓ cup Cabernet Sauvignon or dry red wine
2 tablespoons water
1 tablespoon margarine or butter
1 medium onion, cut into wedges
1 small green or red bell pepper, cut into strips
Hot cooked rice

Place pork slices, ½ cup wine, the oil and garlic in plastic bag. Fasten bag securely. Refrigerate 1 hour.

Remove pork; discard wine mixture. Cover and grill pork 5 to 6 inches from medium coals, turning once, until pork is done and no longer pink in center, about 15 minutes.

Heat remaining ingredients except rice to boiling; reduce heat. Simmer uncovered, stirring occasionally, until vegetables are crisp-tender, about 5 minutes. Pour vegetable mixture over pork; serve with rice.

4 servings.

BROILED PORK WITH VEGETABLE SAUCE: Prepare as directed above except set oven control to broil. Place pork on rack in broiler pan. Broil with tops about 4 inches from heat until pork is done and no longer pink in center, 15 to 18 minutes. Continue as directed above.

Grilled slices of pork tenderloin have incomparable out-of-doors flavor. But if the weather is less than perfect, you can broil the tenderloin to moist perfection.

Spinach Lasagne with White Sauce

8 ounces bulk Italian sausage, crumbled
4 ounces smoked chicken or turkey, finely chopped
1 large onion, finely chopped
1 medium stalk celery, finely chopped
1 medium carrot, finely shredded
2 cloves garlic, finely chopped
1¾ cups water

¾ cup Pinot Noir or dry red wine
⅓ cup tomato paste
½ teaspoon Italian herb seasoning
⅛ teaspoon pepper
Dash of ground nutmeg
2 cups shredded mozzarella cheese (8 ounces)
1½ cups grated Parmesan cheese
¼ cup snipped parsley
White Sauce (below)
12 spinach lasagne noodles, uncooked

Cook and stir sausage in 12-inch skillet or 4-quart Dutch oven until light brown; drain. Stir in chicken, onion, celery, carrot, garlic, water, wine, tomato paste, Italian seasoning, pepper and nutmeg. Heat to boiling; reduce heat. Simmer uncovered 1 hour, stirring occasionally.

Toss mozzarella and Parmesan cheeses and parsley; reserve ½ cup. Prepare White Sauce. Prepare noodles as directed on package: drain.

Heat oven to 350°. Spread 1 cup of the sausage mixture in ungreased rectangular baking dish, 13 × 9 × 2 inches. Layer with 3 lasagne noodles, half of the White Sauce, half of the cheese mixture, 3 lasagne noodles and half of the remaining sausage mixture; repeat. Sprinkle with reserved cheese mixture. Bake uncovered until hot and bubbly, about 35 minutes. Let stand 10 minutes before cutting.

12 servings.

WHITE SAUCE

⅓ cup margarine or butter
⅓ cup all-purpose flour
1 teaspoon salt
Dash of ground nutmeg
3 cups milk

Heat margarine over low heat until melted. Stir in flour, salt and nutmeg. Cook over low heat, stirring constantly, until smooth and bubbly; remove from heat. Stir in milk. Heat to boiling, stirring constantly. Boil and stir 1 minute; cover and keep warm. (If sauce thickens, beat in small amount of milk. Sauce should be the consistency of heavy cream.)

*H*ere is the formula for a traditional northern Italian lasagne. The Bolognese are famous for their beloved lasagne, made with green spinach pasta and creamy white sauce. This is a dish where the zest of Parmesan cheese, at its best freshly grated, really comes through, enhancing the smoky flavor of the chicken.

Lamb Shanks with Mint-Yogurt Sauce

4 lamb shanks (about 1 pound each)
2 tablespoons vegetable oil
1 cup Grey Riesling or dry white wine
1 tablespoon instant chicken bouillon
1 large onion, sliced
1 tablespoon cornstarch
1 tablespoon cold water
1 cup lemon-flavored yogurt
1 tablespoon snipped fresh mint leaves or 1 teaspoon dried mint leaves

Cook lamb shanks in oil in 4-quart Dutch oven, turning occasionally, until brown; drain. Add wine, bouillon (dry) and onion. Heat to boiling; reduce heat. Cover and simmer, turning occasionally, until tender, about 2 hours.

Remove lamb to warm platter; keep warm. Drain broth; skim off fat if necessary. Return 1 cup broth to Dutch oven. Mix cornstarch and water; gradually stir into broth. Heat to boiling, stirring constantly. Boil and stir 1 minute. Stir in yogurt and mint leaves; heat just until hot. Serve sauce with lamb.

4 servings.

Ground Lamb and Eggplant

1 medium eggplant (1½ to 2 pounds)
½ teaspoon salt
½ cup all-purpose flour
Vegetable oil
1 pound ground lamb
1 medium onion, chopped
2 tablespoons margarine or butter
1 can (8 ounces) tomato sauce
1 cup Gamay Beaujolais or dry red wine
2 tablespoons snipped parsley
¼ teaspoon pepper
¼ teaspoon ground nutmeg
1 egg, beaten

½ cup grated Kefalotyri, Parmesan or Romano cheese
¼ cup dry bread crumbs
3 tablespoons margarine or butter
3 tablespoons all-purpose flour
½ teaspoon salt
¼ teaspoon ground nutmeg
1¾ cups milk
2 eggs, slightly beaten
¼ cup grated Kefalotyri, Parmesan or Romano cheese
¼ cup dry bread crumbs
4 tablespoons grated Kefalotyri, Parmesan or Romano cheese

Pare eggplant; cut crosswise into ¼-inch slices. Sprinkle slices with ½ teaspoon salt. Coat with ½ cup flour; shake off excess. Heat 2 tablespoons oil in 10-inch skillet. Cook several eggplant slices in hot oil until golden brown on both sides. Repeat with remaining slices, adding more oil when necessary; drain.

Cook and stir ground lamb and onion in 2 tablespoons margarine in 10-inch skillet until lamb is brown. Stir in tomato sauce, wine, parsley, pepper and ¼ teaspoon nutmeg. Cook uncovered until half of liquid is absorbed, about 20 minutes. Stir in 1 beaten egg, ½ cup cheese and ¼ cup dry bread crumbs. Remove from heat.

Heat oven to 375°. Heat 3 tablespoons margarine in 2-quart saucepan until melted. Stir in 3 tablespoons flour, ½ teaspoon salt and ¼ teaspoon nutmeg. Cook over low heat, stirring constantly, until mixture is smooth and bubbly. Stir in milk. Heat to boiling, stirring constantly. Stir small amount of hot milk mixture into 2 slightly beaten eggs. Stir egg mixture into hot mixture in saucepan. Stir in ¼ cup cheese.

Grease rectangular baking dish, 12 × 7½ × 2 inches, or square pan, 9 × 9 × 2 inches. Sprinkle ¼ cup dry bread crumbs evenly in dish. Arrange half of the eggplant slices in dish; cover with lamb mixture. Sprinkle with 2 tablespoons of the cheese; top with remaining eggplant slices. Pour sauce over eggplant slices; sprinkle with remaining 2 tablespoons cheese. Bake uncovered until golden brown and bubbly, about 45 minutes. Remove from oven; let stand 20 minutes before serving.

6 servings.

*O*riginally a Rumanian specialty, Ground Lamb and Eggplant *(Moussaka)* is a popular dish in Greece and throughout the Near East. The exotic blend of seasonings and the special affinity of eggplant for lamb make this an exceptionally delicious casserole. Wine, in this case Gamay Beaujolais, is stirred into the skillet after the meat has been partly cooked. This encourages the browned bits of lamb, stuck in the bottom of the pan, to dissolve into a deep-flavored sauce.

CHAPTER 4

Ways with Eggs and Cheese

Pickled Eggs and Beets with Smoked Fish

6 hard-cooked eggs, peeled
1 small onion, thinly sliced
1 can (8¼ ounces) sliced beets, drained (reserve liquid)
1 cup cider vinegar
½ cup Ruby Port or sweet red wine
2 tablespoons sugar
¼ teaspoon salt
4 whole cloves
8 ounces smoked fish or pickled herring
Leaf lettuce
⅓ cup vegetable oil
Freshly ground pepper

Place peeled eggs, onion and beets in deep glass bowl or jar. Mix reserved beet liquid, vinegar, port, sugar, salt and cloves; pour over egg mixture. Cover and refrigerate at least 2 days.

Drain, reserving ⅓ cup wine mixture. Slice eggs. Arrange eggs, beets, onions and smoked fish on lettuce. Shake reserved wine mixture, the oil and pepper in tightly covered container. Serve with eggs. Sprinkle with freshly ground pepper if desired.

4 servings.

*C*hoose a deep bowl or jar for marinating the eggs and vegetables. That way, they will be thoroughly covered with the pickling liquid and will take on the same degree of color, a brilliant sunset pink.

Puffy Apple Omelet

2 tablespoons margarine or butter
2 medium unpared tart apples, cut into ½-inch slices
¼ cup French Colombard or dry white wine
6 eggs, separated
¼ cup French Colombard or dry white wine
½ teaspoon salt
¼ cup sliced green onions (with tops)

Heat oven to 325°. Heat margarine in 10-inch ovenproof skillet over medium heat until melted. Stir in apple slices and ¼ cup wine. Cook uncovered over medium heat, stirring occasionally, just until liquid has evaporated, about 10 minutes.

While apples cook, beat egg whites, ¼ cup wine and the salt in large bowl on high speed until stiff but not dry. Beat egg yolks in medium bowl on high speed until very thick and lemon colored, about 3 minutes. Fold beaten egg yolks and green onions into egg whites.

Pour egg mixture over apple mixture in skillet; level surface gently. Cook uncovered over low heat until puffy and light brown on edge, about 5 minutes. (Lift omelet carefully at edge to judge color.)

Carefully place skillet in oven. Bake uncovered until knife inserted in center comes out clean, about 12 minutes. Invert on heatproof serving plate if desired. Cut into wedges.

4 servings.

Puffy Apple Omelet

Smoked Salmon–Broccoli Soufflé

1 small onion, chopped
¼ cup margarine or butter
¼ cup all-purpose flour
⅛ teaspoon pepper
½ cup milk
½ cup Chardonnay or dry white wine
3 eggs, separated
¼ teaspoon cream of tartar
1 package (10 ounces) frozen chopped broccoli, thawed and well
  drained
4 ounces smoked salmon, flaked or chopped

Heat oven to 350°. Butter 1-quart soufflé dish or casserole. Cook and stir onion in margarine in 2-quart saucepan over low heat until tender. Stir in flour and pepper. Cook over low heat, stirring constantly, until bubbly; remove from heat. Stir in milk until blended; stir in wine. Heat to boiling, stirring constantly. Boil and stir 1 minute; remove from heat.

Beat egg whites and cream of tartar in medium bowl on high speed until stiff but not dry. Beat egg yolks in small bowl on high speed until very thick and lemon colored, about 3 minutes; stir into wine mixture.

Stir about one-fourth of the beaten egg whites into wine mixture. Fold wine mixture into remaining egg-white mixture. Gently fold in broccoli and salmon.

Carefully pour into soufflé dish. Bake uncovered until knife inserted halfway between center and edge comes out clean, 60 to 65 minutes. Gently divide soufflé into portions, using 2 forks. Serve immediately.

4 servings.

Sherried Eggs and Asparagus

¼ cup Dry Sherry or dry white wine
1 tablespoon margarine or butter
6 hard-cooked eggs, peeled and cut lengthwise into halves
1 cup half-and-half
¼ teaspoon salt
⅛ teaspoon freshly ground pepper
1 tablespoon all-purpose flour
2 tablespoons Dry Sherry or dry white wine
4 slices whole wheat bread, toasted
1 package (10 ounces) frozen asparagus spears or 1 pound fresh
  asparagus, cooked

Heat ¼ cup sherry and the margarine in 10-inch skillet over medium heat until margarine is melted. Place peeled eggs, cut sides down, in skillet; reduce heat. Simmer uncovered until heated through, about 5 minutes. Remove eggs; keep warm. Stir half-and-half, salt and pepper into sherry mixture in skillet. Shake flour and 2 tablespoons wine in tightly covered container; stir into half-and-half mixture. Heat to boiling over medium heat, stirring constantly. Boil and stir 1 minute.

Cut each slice bread into 4 triangles. Arrange 3 egg halves, cut sides up, and several asparagus spears on each serving plate. Place 4 toast triangles on each plate. Spoon some sauce over eggs. Serve with remaining sauce.

4 servings.

*T*he addition of Dry Sherry transforms these saucy boiled eggs into a debonair late breakfast or luncheon. A fortified wine, sherry is delicious in almost any creamy sauce, whether sweet or savory. Crisp-tender asparagus spears, at their best fresh and lightly steamed, are a finishing touch of elegance.

Sherried Eggs and Asparagus

Cooking with American Wine

Herbed Crab Custards

1/4 cup sliced green onions (with tops)
2 tablespoons margarine or butter
1 cup dairy sour cream
1/4 cup Chenin Blanc or dry white wine
1/4 cup milk
1 teaspoon snipped fresh tarragon leaves or 1/4 teaspoon dried
    tarragon leaves
1/2 teaspoon salt
4 eggs
1 package (6 ounces) frozen crabmeat, thawed and well drained,
    or 6 ounces imitation crabmeat, cut into 1/2-inch pieces

Heat oven to 350°. Cook and stir green onions in margarine
in 1-quart saucepan over medium heat until tender;
remove from heat.

Beat remaining ingredients except crabmeat until smooth;
stir in onions and crabmeat. Pour mixture into 4 ungreased
10-ounce custard cups. Place cups in rectangular pan, 13
× 9 × 2 inches, on oven rack. Pour very hot water into pan
to within 1/2 inch of tops of cups.

Bake until knife inserted halfway between center and edge
comes out clean, 30 to 35 minutes. Serve immediately.
Refrigerate any remaining custards.

4 servings.

Vegetable Platter
with Wine-Cheese Sauce

2 cups cauliflower flowerets
2 small zucchini, cut into 1/2-inch slices
20 Chinese pea pods
1 red bell pepper, cut into 1/2-inch strips
2 tablespoons margarine or butter
2 tablespoons all-purpose flour
1/8 teaspoon salt
1/8 teaspoon ground nutmeg
Dash of pepper
1 cup half-and-half
1 cup shredded natural Swiss cheese (4 ounces)
1/4 cup Chenin Blanc or dry white wine
4 croissants, split and toasted

Place steamer basket in ½ inch water in 4-quart Dutch oven (water should not touch bottom of basket). Place vegetables in basket. Cover tightly and heat to boiling; reduce heat. Steam until vegetables are crisp-tender, about 12 minutes.

Heat margarine in 2-quart saucepan over low heat until melted. Stir in flour, salt, nutmeg and pepper. Cook over low heat, stirring constantly, until mixture is smooth and bubbly; remove from heat. Stir in half-and-half. Heat to boiling, stirring constantly. Boil and stir 1 minute. Stir in cheese and wine until cheese is melted.

Arrange vegetables on serving platter. Pour about half of the sauce over vegetables. Serve with remaining sauce and the toasted croissants.

4 servings.

Grilled Port-Cheese Sandwiches

1 package (8 ounces) cream cheese, softened
¼ cup Ruby Port or sweet red wine
2 cups shredded Cheddar cheese (8 ounces)
20 slices French bread, each ½-inch thick
Margarine or butter, softened

Mix cream cheese and wine, using spoon, until well blended. Stir in Cheddar cheese. For each sandwich, spread about 3 tablespoons of the cheese mixture evenly on 1 slice bread. Top with second slice. Spread top slices of bread with margarine.

Place 5 sandwiches, margarine sides down, in 10-inch skillet. Spread top slices of bread with margarine. Cook uncovered over medium heat until golden brown, 3 to 4 minutes; turn. Cook until golden brown and cheese is warm, about 2 minutes longer. Repeat with remaining sandwiches. Serve with fresh fruit if desired.

10 sandwiches.

*T*o toast croissants: Split and place, cut surface up, on a broiler pan. Broil until golden brown. Wrap in foil to keep them warm.

Cream of Cheese Soup

3 green onions (with tops), thinly sliced
½ cup thinly sliced celery
2 tablespoons margarine or butter
⅔ cup process cheese spread
1¼ cups water
½ cup half-and-half
1 teaspoon instant chicken bouillon
⅛ teaspoon ground nutmeg
⅓ cup Sémillon or dry white wine
Seasoned croutons or popped popcorn

Cook and stir green onions and celery in margarine in 3-quart saucepan over medium heat until onions are tender, about 8 minutes. Stir in remaining ingredients except wine and croutons.

Heat to boiling over medium heat, stirring constantly; stir in wine. Heat to boiling. Boil and stir 1 minute. Sprinkle with croutons and, if desired, paprika.

3 servings.

Cheese Fondue

2 cups shredded natural Swiss cheese (8 ounces)*
2 cups shredded Gruyère cheese (8 ounces)
2 tablespoons all-purpose flour
1 clove garlic, cut into halves
2 cups Sauvignon Blanc or dry white wine
1 tablespoon lemon juice
3 tablespoons kirsch
French bread, cut into 1-inch cubes

Place cheeses and flour in plastic bag; fasten bag securely. Shake until cheese is coated. Rub garlic on bottom and sides of 3-quart saucepan; add wine. Heat over low heat just until bubbles rise to surface (do not boil); stir in lemon juice.

Gradually add cheeses, about ½ cup at a time, stirring constantly with wooden spoon over low heat until cheeses are melted. Stir in kirsch. Remove to earthenware fondue dish; keep warm over low heat and serve with bread cubes for dipping.

4 servings.

* Swiss cheese should be aged at least 6 months.

*V*elvety Cream of Cheese Soup would be warming fare on a chilly autumn day. With the simple addition of a green salad, it makes an elegant lunch.

*C*heese fondue is said to come from the French-speaking region of Switzerland (the name *fondue* is derived from the French word for "to melt"). This simple fondue gets its classic flavor from kirsch, a clear spirit distilled from fermented cherries.

Cream of Cheese Soup

Cooking with American Wine

Cheese-topped Onion Soup

2 tablespoons margarine or butter
1 teaspoon sugar
4 medium onions, sliced
1½ cups water
1 cup Gamay Beaujolais or dry red wine
⅛ teaspoon pepper
1 bay leaf
1 can (10½ ounces) condensed beef broth
4 slices French bread, each ¾ to 1 inch thick
2 cups shredded Gruyère or natural Swiss cheese (8 ounces)
¼ cup grated Parmesan cheese

Heat margarine in 3-quart saucepan over low heat until melted. Stir in sugar and onions. Cook uncovered, stirring frequently, until onions are deep golden brown, about 35 minutes.

Stir in remaining ingredients except bread and cheeses. Heat to boiling; reduce heat. Cover and simmer 15 minutes. Remove bay leaf. Keep warm.

Set oven control to broil. Broil French bread with tops about 5 inches from heat until golden brown, 1 to 2 minutes; turn bread over. Broil until golden brown. Place 1 slice bread in each of 4 heatproof bowls or 10-ounce casseroles. Pour soup over bread; top with Gruyère cheese. Sprinkle with Parmesan cheese.

Place bowls on cookie sheet. Broil with tops about 5 inches from heat just until cheese is melted and light brown, about 3 minutes. Serve with additional French bread if desired.

4 servings.

Sausage and Eggs with Cheese Sauce

6 hard-cooked eggs, peeled
2 tablespoons all-purpose flour
½ cup dry bread crumbs
¼ teaspoon ground sage
1 egg
12 ounces bulk pork sausage
Cheese Sauce (right)

Heat oven to 400°. Coat each peeled egg with flour. Mix remaining ingredients except Cheese Sauce; divide mixture into 6 equal portions. Pat each portion into a flat 5-inch

*T*hese hard-cooked eggs coated with a sausage mixture may have originated in Scotland as breakfast food. "Scotch eggs" are snacking fare throughout Britain, as popular in English pubs as pretzels are in some American cafés. (Some say the recipe is really an English invention; these eggs stretch the meat bill and so were haughtily dubbed "Scotch" for the legendary Scottish sense of thrift.)

oval or round patty; mold 1 patty around each egg. Bake in ungreased jelly roll pan, 15½ × 10½ × 1 inch, until deep golden brown, 20 to 25 minutes. Serve with Cheese Sauce.

6 servings.

CHEESE SAUCE

2 tablespoons margarine or butter
2 tablespoons all-purpose flour
⅛ teaspoon salt
⅛ teaspoon paprika
¾ cup milk
1 cup shredded process American cheese (4 ounces)
¼ cup Pinot Noir Blanc or dry white wine
1 tablespoon snipped parsley

Heat margarine in 1-quart saucepan over low heat until melted. Stir in flour, salt and paprika. Cook over low heat, stirring constantly, until smooth and bubbly; remove from heat. Stir in milk. Heat to boiling, stirring constantly. Boil and stir 1 minute. Stir in remaining ingredients until cheese is melted.

Smoked Cheese and French Bread Bake

½ loaf (1-pound size) French bread
1½ cups shredded smoked Gouda cheese (6 ounces)
1 cup finely chopped fully cooked smoked ham (about 4 ounces)
4 green onions (with tops), sliced
4 eggs
⅓ cup Sémillon or dry white wine
1 tablespoon Dijon-style mustard
¼ teaspoon red pepper sauce
1 can (14½ ounces) chicken broth
½ cup shredded smoked Gouda cheese (2 ounces)

Heat oven to 325°. Cut bread into 16 slices. Arrange 8 slices of bread in ungreased rectangular baking dish, 11 × 7 × 1½ inches. Top with 1½ cups cheese, the ham and green onions. Arrange remaining bread on top. Beat remaining ingredients except ½ cup cheese; pour mixture over bread.

Bake uncovered until knife inserted in center comes out clean, about 1 hour. Sprinkle ½ cup cheese over top. Let stand 10 minutes before serving.

8 servings.

*S*moked Gouda cheese gives this puffed, golden casserole a sophisticated flavor. Dense Gouda cheese is a Dutch invention, quickly recognized in its red or yellow waxy casing.

Cheesy Spaghetti Toss

1 package (16 ounces) thin spaghetti
½ pound bacon, cut into ½-inch pieces
½ cup Chardonnay or dry white wine
½ cup grated Romano or Parmesan cheese
3 eggs, well beaten
½ cup grated Romano or Parmesan cheese
Freshly ground pepper

Cook spaghetti as directed on package; drain but do not rinse. Return to pan.

Cook and stir bacon over medium heat in separate pan until almost crisp. Remove bacon, using slotted spoon; reserve bacon.

Stir wine into bacon fat. Heat to boiling. Boil and stir 3 minutes. Pour wine mixture over spaghetti; add bacon. Add ½ cup cheese and the eggs; toss over low heat until egg adheres to spaghetti and appears cooked. Serve with remaining cheese and freshly ground pepper.

4 servings.

Blue Cheese Soufflé

2 tablespoons dry bread crumbs
¼ cup margarine or butter
¼ cup all-purpose flour
⅛ teaspoon pepper
½ cup milk
½ cup Chardonnay or dry white wine
½ package (4-ounce size) blue cheese, crumbled (about ½ cup)
3 eggs, separated
¼ teaspoon cream of tartar
½ cup dairy sour cream
¼ cup whipping cream

Heat oven to 350°. Butter 1-quart soufflé dish or casserole. Make a 4-inch-wide band of triple-thickness aluminum foil 2 inches longer than circumference of dish; butter 1 side of foil. Secure foil band, buttered side in, around outside edge of dish and sprinkle evenly with bread crumbs.

Heat margarine in 2-quart saucepan over low heat until melted. Stir in flour and pepper. Cook over low heat, stirring constantly, until smooth and bubbly; remove from heat. Stir in milk until blended; stir in wine. Heat to boiling, stirring constantly. Boil and stir 1 minute. Stir in cheese until melted; remove from heat.

*S*erved with apple and pear slices and a loaf of warm French bread, this soufflé is perfect for a luncheon or after-theater rendezvous. Blue cheeses vary tremendously in character. Try a Danish-style blue for mellow flavor, French roquefort for subtlety or a true French *bleu* for mouth-watering sharpness.

Cooking with American Wine

Beat egg whites and cream of tartar in medium bowl on high speed until stiff but not dry. Beat egg yolks in small bowl on high speed until very thick and lemon colored, about 3 minutes; stir into cheese mixture. Stir about one-fourth of the beaten egg whites into cheese mixture. Fold cheese mixture into remaining egg whites.

Carefully pour into soufflé dish. Bake uncovered until knife inserted halfway between center and edge comes out clean, 50 to 60 minutes. Mix sour cream and whipping cream. Carefully remove foil band, and divide soufflé into portions, using 2 forks. Serve immediately with sour cream mixture. Sprinkle with chopped tomato and avocado or chopped apples and toasted almonds if desired.

3 servings.

Chicken-Gruyère Quiche

Pastry for 9-inch one-crust pie
6 slices bacon, cut into ½-inch pieces
1 small onion, chopped
1 cup cut-up cooked chicken
1 cup shredded Gruyère or Swiss cheese (4 ounces)
2 tablespoons snipped parsley
5 eggs
1¼ cups half-and-half
½ cup Grey Riesling or dry white wine
¼ teaspoon pepper
⅛ teaspoon salt

Place oven rack in lowest position. Heat oven to 425°. Fold pastry into fourths; unfold and ease into ungreased quiche dish, 9 × 1½ inches, or pie plate, 9 × 1¼ inches, pressing firmly against bottom and sides. Trim overhanging edge of pastry 1 inch from rim of dish. Fold and roll pastry under to make it even with dish; flute edge.

Cook and stir bacon over medium heat until almost crisp; stir in onion. Cook until onion is tender; drain.

Sprinkle chicken, cheese and parsley in pastry. Beat remaining ingredients until blended; stir in bacon mixture. Place quiche dish on oven rack; pour egg-bacon mixture over cheese. Bake 15 minutes.

Reduce oven temperature to 300°. Bake until knife inserted in center comes out clean, about 30 minutes longer. Let stand 10 minutes before cutting.

6 servings.

CHAPTER 5

Elegant Endings

Peaches in Wine

¹/₄ cup sugar
¹/₄ cup White Port or sweet white wine
1 tablespoon lemon juice
3 medium peaches, peeled and sliced

Heat sugar, port and lemon juice over medium heat until sugar is dissolved; pour over peaches. Cover and refrigerate, stirring occasionally, until chilled, about 1 hour.

4 servings.

Spicy Fruit Compote

2-inch cinnamon stick
6 whole cloves
¹/₄ cup sugar
¹/₂ cup Ruby Port or sweet red wine
¹/₂ cup water
2 tablespoons lemon juice
1 package (11 ounces) mixed dried fruit
2 bananas, sliced

Tie cinnamon stick and cloves in cheesecloth bag. Heat cheesecloth bag, sugar, port, water and lemon juice to boiling in 2-quart saucepan. Stir in dried fruit. Heat to boiling; reduce heat. Simmer uncovered, stirring occasionally, until fruit is plump and tender, 10 to 15 minutes. Refrigerate uncovered, at least 3 hours but no longer than 24 hours, stirring occasionally.

Remove and discard cheesecloth bag. Stir bananas into fruit mixture until coated with syrup. Drain fruit, reserving syrup. Serve fruit with some of the syrup.

5 servings.

*P*ort is an ideal background flavor for this compote. It is smooth enough to enhance the taste of the dried fruits but rich enough not to be overwhelmed by the medley.

Pears Poached in Red Wine

6 small pears, pared, cored and cut into halves
Juice of 1 lemon
1⅓ cups sugar
2 cups Pinot Noir or dry red wine
2-inch cinnamon stick

Dip pears in lemon juice. Heat sugar, wine and cinnamon stick in 10-inch skillet, stirring constantly, until sugar is dissolved and mixture boils; reduce heat. Add pears. Simmer uncovered until pears are soft but not mushy when pierced with sharp knife, about 15 minutes.

Cool pears in syrup until lukewarm; remove cinnamon stick. Serve warm, or refrigerate until cold.

6 servings.

Orange-Port Soufflé

½ cup sugar
¾ cup White Port or sweet white wine
¾ cup orange juice
¼ cup water
⅛ teaspoon salt
2 envelopes unflavored gelatin
4 eggs, separated
2 teaspoons grated orange peel
¾ cup sugar
2 cups whipping cream
2 to 3 tablespoons White Port or sweet white wine
½ cup orange marmalade

Make a 4-inch-wide band of triple-thickness aluminum foil 2 inches longer than circumference of 1½-quart soufflé dish. Secure band around edge of dish.

Mix ½ cup sugar, the port, orange juice, water, salt and gelatin in 1½-quart saucepan. Beat egg yolks slightly; stir into gelatin mixture. Heat just to boiling over medium heat, stirring constantly; remove from heat. Stir in orange peel.

Refrigerate, stirring occasionally, just until mixture mounds slightly when dropped from a spoon, 20 to 30 minutes. (If mixture becomes too thick, place pan in bowl of hot water; stir constantly until of proper consistency.)

Beat egg whites in large bowl until foamy. Beat in ¾ cup sugar, 1 tablespoon at a time; continue beating until stiff

*P*ears poached in a red wine syrup turn a pretty shade of crimson. In the winter they are especially nice served still warm, with ice cream. Serve them thoroughly chilled in the summer, and pass a plate of thin, crisp cookies.

Cooking with American Wine

and glossy. Do not underbeat. Fold gelatin mixture into egg whites.

Beat whipping cream in chilled medium bowl until stiff. Fold into egg-white mixture. Carefully turn into soufflé dish. Refrigerate until set, about 8 hours.

Just before serving, run knife around inside of foil band and carefully remove band. Stir 2 to 3 tablespoons port into marmalade, and serve with soufflé. Refrigerate any remaining soufflé immediately.

12 servings.

Fudge Soufflé

½ cup sugar
1¾ cups Ruby Port or sweet red wine
¼ teaspoon salt
2 envelopes unflavored gelatin
6 eggs, separated
1 package (12 ounces) semisweet chocolate chips
½ cup sugar
1½ cups whipping cream

Make a 3-inch-wide band of double-thickness aluminum foil 2 inches longer than circumference of 1½-quart soufflé dish. Secure band around edge of dish.

Mix ½ cup sugar, the port, salt and gelatin in 2-quart saucepan. Beat egg yolks slightly; stir yolks and chocolate chips into gelatin mixture. Heat just to boiling over medium heat, stirring constantly; remove from heat.

Refrigerate, stirring occasionally, just until mixture mounds slightly when dropped from a spoon, 20 to 30 minutes. (If mixture becomes too thick, place pan in bowl of hot water; stir constantly until of proper consistency.)

Beat egg whites in large bowl until foamy. Beat in ½ cup sugar, 1 tablespoon at a time; continue beating until stiff and glossy. Do not underbeat. Fold gelatin mixture into egg whites.

Beat whipping cream in chilled medium bowl until stiff. Fold into egg-white mixture. Carefully turn into soufflé dish. Refrigerate until set, about 8 hours.

Just before serving, run knife around inside of foil band and carefully remove band. Refrigerate any remaining soufflé.

12 to 16 servings.

*F*udge Soufflé is a smooth-textured cold soufflé you can stake your reputation on! The flavor, intense and rich, comes from the marvelous blending of wine, chocolate and cream. The foil collar around the rim of the soufflé dish assures the high crown that always elicits *ahs* from around the table.

Water ices—also known as *sorbets, sherbets, glacés* or *granités*—are the simplest frozen desserts, often made of nothing more than fruit juices or purées mixed with a light syrup. For extra flavor, some ices include liqueur or wine, as does our Strawberry-Cabernet Sorbet. Serve this sorbet as a light dessert or offer it between the first and main courses to refresh the palate.

Strawberry-Cabernet Sorbet

1 pint strawberries
½ cup sugar
2 tablespoons lemon juice
1 cup Cabernet Sauvignon or dry red wine

Place strawberries, sugar and lemon juice in food processor workbowl fitted with steel blade or in blender container. Cover and process until smooth. Stir in wine.

Pour into ungreased square baking dish, 8 × 8 × 2 inches. Freeze until firm, at least 8 hours. Let stand at room temperature 5 minutes before serving.

6 to 8 servings.

Wine Custard

4 egg yolks
1 egg
⅓ cup sugar
⅓ cup Cream Sherry or sweet red wine
Dash of salt

Beat egg yolks and egg in small bowl on high speed until thick and lemon colored, about 3 minutes. Gradually beat in sugar, scraping bowl occasionally. Beat in sherry and salt on low speed.

Pour mixture into top of double boiler. (A metal bowl placed over saucepan of simmering water can be substituted for double boiler.) Add enough hot water to bottom of double boiler so that top does not touch water. Cook mixture over medium heat, stirring constantly, until slightly thickened, about 5 minutes. (Water in double boiler should simmer but not boil.) Remove from heat. Serve immediately.

4 servings.

Strawberry-Cabernet Sorbet

Raspberry-Custard Bowl

½ cup sugar
3 tablespoons cornstarch
¼ teaspoon salt
3 cups milk
½ cup Dry Sherry or dry white wine
3 egg yolks, beaten
3 tablespoons margarine or butter, softened
1 tablespoon vanilla
2 packages (3 ounces each) ladyfingers
½ cup red raspberry preserves
1 package (16 ounces) frozen unsweetened red raspberries,
*   partially thawed*
1 package (3 ounces) slivered almonds, toasted
1 cup whipping cream
2 tablespoons sugar

Mix ½ cup sugar, the cornstarch and salt in 3-quart saucepan; gradually stir in milk and sherry. Heat to boiling over medium heat, stirring constantly. Boil and stir 1 minute. Gradually stir about half of the hot mixture into egg yolks. Stir egg yolks back into hot mixture in saucepan. Boil and stir 1 minute; remove from heat. Stir in margarine and vanilla until margarine is melted. Cover and refrigerate at least 3 hours.

Split ladyfingers lengthwise into halves; spread each half with raspberry preserves. Reserve about 10 raspberries for garnish if desired. Layer one-fourth of the ladyfingers (cut sides up), 2 tablespoons of the almonds, half of the remaining raspberries and half of the custard in 2½- to 3-quart serving bowl; repeat layers.

Arrange remaining ladyfingers upright around edge of bowl, with cut sides toward center. (It may be necessary to gently ease ladyfingers down into custard about 1 inch so that they stand upright.) Cover and refrigerate at least 30 minutes but no longer than 4 hours.

Beat whipping cream and 2 tablespoons sugar in chilled bowl until stiff; spread over top of dessert. Sprinkle with remaining almonds, and garnish with reserved raspberries.

8 to 10 servings.

*A*s English as the Union Jack, trifle (Raspberry-Custard Bowl) is one of many custard dishes favored by the British. We've trimmed preparation time by using ready-made ladyfingers, a boon for busy cooks. Trifle is best served in a clear glass bowl so that the richly colored layers are visible. Spectacular!

Sherried Bread Pudding

1¼ cups milk
¼ cup margarine or butter
2 eggs, slightly beaten
¾ cup dried fruit snack mix (peaches, apricots, apples and
*   raisins)**
½ cup sugar
⅓ cup Cream Sherry or sweet red wine
½ teaspoon ground nutmeg
¼ teaspoon salt
4 cups 1-inch French bread cubes (about 5 slices)
Sherry Cream (below)

Heat oven to 350°. Heat milk and margarine over medium heat until margarine is melted and milk is scalded. Mix eggs, snack mix, sugar, sherry, nutmeg and salt in ungreased 1½-quart casserole; stir in bread cubes. Pour in milk mixture. Place casserole in pan of very hot water (1 inch deep).

Bake uncovered until knife inserted 1 inch from edge of casserole comes out clean, 40 to 45 minutes. Serve warm with Sherry Cream.

8 servings.

* ½ cup cut-up dried mixed fruit and ¼ cup golden raisins can be substituted for the dried fruit snack mix.

SHERRY CREAM

½ cup whipping cream
1 tablespoon Cream Sherry or sweet red wine

Beat whipping cream in chilled small bowl until stiff. Gently stir in sherry.

Sherried Bread Pudding is a stout and comforting dessert, conjuring images of cosy chairs and fireside chats. This pudding boasts chunks of crusty French bread, sweet bits of dried fruit and the warm, mellow taste of Cream Sherry.

Honey-Wine Cranberry Tart

Cookie Crust (below)
1/3 cup orange marmalade
1/2 cup coarsely chopped walnuts
1 envelope unflavored gelatin
1/4 cup cold water
1 cup Sauvignon Blanc or dry white wine
1/2 cup honey
1 package (12 ounces) fresh cranberries
Sweetened whipped cream

Heat oven to 375°. Prepare Cookie Crust. Press in bottom and 1½ inches up side of ungreased springform pan, 9 × 3 inches. Bake until crust is set and light brown, 18 to 20 minutes. Spread orange marmalade on bottom; sprinkle with nuts.

Sprinkle gelatin on cold water in 3-quart saucepan. Let stand until gelatin is softened, about 5 minutes. Stir in remaining ingredients except whipped cream. Heat to boiling; reduce heat slightly. Boil uncovered 5 minutes. Cool 15 minutes.

Pour cranberry mixture over nuts in crust. Cover and refrigerate until chilled, at least 4 hours. Remove side of pan. Serve with sweetened whipped cream.

8 to 10 servings.

COOKIE CRUST

1 3/4 cups all-purpose flour
1/2 cup powdered sugar
3/4 cup margarine or butter, softened

Mix all ingredients until crumbly; mix with hands until dough forms.

*W*eeks after Thanksgiving has come and gone, half-empty bags of these scarlet berries sit neglected at the back of the refrigerator. Cranberries aren't just for holidays! Honey-Wine Cranberry Tart features tart cranberries with crunchy walnuts and a hint of orange.

Honey-Wine Cranberry Tart

Red Wine Apple Pie

5 cups thinly sliced, pared tart cooking apples
¾ cup sugar
¼ cup Ruby Port or sweet red wine
1 tablespoon lemon juice
¼ cup all-purpose flour
2 tablespoons sugar
⅛ teaspoon salt
3 tablespoons margarine or butter
Cheese Pastry (below)

Place apples, ¾ cup sugar, the port and lemon juice in 3-quart saucepan. Cover and cook over medium heat, stirring occasionally, just until apples are tender, 7 to 8 minutes.

Mix flour, 2 tablespoons sugar and the salt; stir into apple mixture. Heat to boiling, stirring constantly. Boil and stir 1 minute; remove from heat. Stir in margarine. Cool to room temperature.

Heat oven to 425°. Prepare Cheese Pastry. Gather pastry into a ball; divide into halves, and shape into 2 flattened rounds on lightly floured cloth-covered surface. Roll 1 round 2 inches larger than inverted 8-inch pie plate, using floured cloth-covered rolling pin. Fold pastry into fourths; unfold and ease into pie plate, pressing firmly against bottom and side.

Turn apple mixture into pastry-lined pie plate. Trim overhanging edge of pastry ½ inch from rim of plate. Roll other round of pastry. Fold into fourths; cut slits so steam can escape.

Place pastry over filling and unfold. Trim overhanging edge 1 inch from rim of plate. Fold and roll top edge under lower edge, pressing on rim to seal; flute edge. Cover edge with 2- to 3-inch-wide strip of aluminum foil to prevent excessive browning; remove foil during last 15 minutes of baking. Bake until crust is brown and juice begins to bubble through slits in crust, 50 to 55 minutes.

6 servings.

CHEESE PASTRY

2 cups all-purpose flour
1 cup shredded Cheddar cheese (4 ounces)
1 teaspoon salt
⅔ cup plus 2 tablespoons shortening
4 to 5 tablespoons cold water

*W*e've combined the simplicity of fruit, wine and cheese into a wonderful American favorite: old-fashioned apple pie. The wine sharpens the taste of the apples, and the Cheddar cheese in the golden crust accents the tartness of the filling.

Mix flour, cheese and salt in large bowl; cut in shortening until particles are size of small peas. Sprinkle in water, 1 tablespoon at a time, tossing with fork until all flour is moistened and pastry almost cleans side of bowl (1 to 2 teaspoons water can be added if necessary).

Almond Cream Pie

1½ cups vanilla wafer crumbs (about 33 wafers)
¼ cup finely chopped slivered almonds
¼ cup margarine or butter, melted
¼ cup sugar
¼ cup all-purpose flour
⅛ teaspoon salt
1 envelope unflavored gelatin
⅔ cup milk
½ cup White Port or sweet white wine
2 eggs, separated
1 cup vanilla wafer crumbs (about 22 wafers)
2 tablespoons White Port or sweet white wine
1 cup whipping cream
¼ teaspoon cream of tartar
1 cup whipping cream
3 tablespoons sugar
Toasted slivered almonds

Heat oven to 350°. Mix 1½ cups wafer crumbs and the chopped almonds; stir in margarine. Press firmly and evenly against bottom and side of ungreased pie plate, 9 × 1¼ inches. Bake 10 minutes; cool.

Mix ¼ cup sugar, the flour, salt and gelatin in 2-quart saucepan. Beat milk, ½ cup port and the egg yolks with hand beater; stir into gelatin mixture. Heat to boiling over low heat, stirring constantly. Place pan in bowl of iced water; stir occasionally until mixture is room temperature, 3 to 5 minutes.

Mix 1 cup wafer crumbs and 2 tablespoons port; stir into gelatin mixture. Beat 1 cup whipping cream in chilled bowl until stiff. Fold into gelatin-crumb mixture. Beat egg whites and cream of tartar until stiff; fold into gelatin-crumb mixture. Spoon into crumb crust. Refrigerate until firm, at least 3½ hours.

Beat 1 cup whipping cream and 3 tablespoons sugar in chilled bowl until stiff; spread over filling. Garnish with slivered almonds. Refrigerate any remaining pie.

6 servings.

Pound Cake with Orange Syrup

1 package (16 ounces) golden pound cake mix
½ cup granulated sugar
½ cup White Port or sweet white wine
½ teaspoon grated orange peel
½ cup orange juice
Powdered sugar

Prepare cake mix as directed on package, except pour batter into greased and floured loaf pan, 9 × 5 × 3 inches. Bake until wooden pick inserted in center comes out clean, 45 to 55 minutes.

Heat remaining ingredients except powdered sugar to boiling in 1½-quart saucepan, stirring constantly. Boil and stir 1 minute; remove from heat.

Cool cake 5 minutes; remove from pan. Place on heatproof serving plate. Pierce top of cake gently several times with fork, inserting tines as far as possible. Spoon syrup over cake; let stand until syrup is absorbed, about 30 minutes. Sprinkle top with powdered sugar. Serve with fresh fruit and whipped cream if desired.

8 servings.

Chocolate-Wine Balls

¼ cup honey
1 package (6 ounces) semisweet chocolate chips
2½ cups vanilla wafer crumbs (about 55 wafers)
2 cups ground walnuts
⅓ cup Ruby Port or sweet red wine
Sugar

Heat honey and chocolate chips in 3-quart saucepan over low heat, stirring constantly, until chocolate is melted; remove from heat. Stir in wafer crumbs, walnuts and port. Shape mixture into 1-inch balls; roll in sugar.

Store in tightly covered container. Let stand several days to blend flavors. Flavor improves with age up to 4 weeks.

About 3½ dozen cookies.

*P*ort, sweet and smooth, was first made in Portugal. The careful pouring of small glasses of port to enjoy after dinner with cheese and nuts became a tradition without which an Edwardian meal was incomplete.

INDEX

Have BETTER HOMES AND GARDENS® magazine delivered to your door. For information, write to;
MR. ROBERT AUSTIN
P.O. BOX4536,
DES MOINES, IA 50336.